MIKE FLYNN

Published by
chosen books

FLEMING H. REVELL COMPANY
OLD TAPPAN, NEW JERSEY

Unless otherwise noted Scripture texts are from the Holy Bible, New International Version, copyright © 1973, 1978, 1984 International Bible Society. Used by permission of Zondervan Bible Publishers.

Scripture quotations identified NAS are from the New American Standard Bible, copyright © The Lockman Foundation 1960, 1962, 1963, 1968, 1971, 1972, 1973, 1975, 1977.

The Scripture quotations contained herein identified RSV are from the Revised Standard Version of the Bible, copyright © 1946, 1952, 1971 by the Division of Christian Education of the National Council of the Churches of Christ in the United States of America, and are used by permission. All rights reserved.

Scripture quotations identified KJV are from the King James Version of the Bible.

The quote on page 159 by S. D. Gordon is taken from *Destined for the Throne* by Paul Bilheimer © 1983 Christian Literature Crusade and used by permission.

The chart on page 93 from *The Gospel of the Kingdom* by G. E. Ladd is used by permission of Wm. B. Eerdmans Pub. Co.

The chart on page 54 was taken from *Christianity and Culture* by Charles Kraft and used by permission of Orbis Books.

The chart on page 141 is used by permission of Robert Fulton.

Library of Congress Cataloging-in-Publication Data

Flynn, Mike, 1940–
    Holy vulnerability/Mike Flynn.
        p.   cm.
    ISBN 0-8007-9168-1
        1. Spiritual life—Anglican authors.   2. Flynn, Mike, 1940–   I. Title.
BV4501.2.F5836   1990
248.4—dc20
                                                                    90-38368
                                                                    CIP

A Chosen Book
Copyright © 1990 by Mike Flynn

Chosen Books are published by
Fleming H. Revell Company
Old Tappan, New Jersey
Printed in the United States of America

To Sue
Kevin
David
Jason
Joel

The author is most grateful to the following persons for their contributions to his life, growth and ministry: To his family for their love, acceptance and encouragement; to the people of St. Jude's Episcopal Church in Burbank for their courage, openness and generosity; to John Wimber for his integrity, leadership and pioneering of biblical ministries; and to countless other friends, intercessors and ministers. God bless you all.

Contents

1
Interacting with God (What This Book Is All About)

I tacked up the ominous poster on the bulletin board of the parish church where I was serving as vicar. This was in 1975, eight years before we moved to St. Jude's Episcopal Church in Burbank, California. At the time I paid little attention to what the poster was saying. But one day I really read the words: *The Seven Warning Signs of Cancer.*

My mouth went dry. "Wait a minute!" I said, counting. "I've got three of the warnings!"

I tend to keep things like that to myself until I get some sort of handle on them. So I stewed about what was going to happen to me for a couple of days, not sleeping well, trying to avoid images of myself lying on a hospital bed hooked up to machines and bottles while my wife, Sue, and our four sons looked on helplessly.

On Thursday of that week I went to the doctor who took a blood sample, telling me that we "would know something in a couple of days." A couple of days, then the bad news! I was quite certain that I was going to die; the only question was how long did I have? At the office I always seemed drowsy, yet that night I couldn't sleep. Sue was breathing deeply beside me but my mind was in high gear. A couple of days

. . . Thursday, Friday, Saturday? Monday was a holiday. I wouldn't know until Tuesday. I lay there, my body reflecting what was going on in my mind, turning this way, then the other.

Suddenly I decided to have it out with God. Emerging gently from our waterbed in order not to awaken Sue, I put on my bathrobe and went into the living room. It was three A.M. Huddling on the couch under the afghan blanket with the Aztec designs, which Sue had knit for me, I began by being honest about my feelings. I had long ago decided that since God knows my feelings anyhow I might just as well talk to Him straight.

"Here I am, Your servant, and You let me get cancer!" I said. "Is this any way to treat friends? I'm thirty-five years old but Sue and I are living from paycheck to paycheck. How're we ever going to pay the medical expenses? What a waste of my education in college and seminary. I'm really just becoming aware of how to minister effectively, and now it's going to end before it really begins. . . ." It all tumbled out of me in machine-gun bursts of fragmented sentences attended by hostile swipes with my hands.

That went on for about fifteen minutes.

After this initial heavenward barrage, I began to land on specific worries related to my early death. One salvo had to do with my sons' educations. Kevin was thirteen at the time, David ten, Jason seven and Joel had just been born. It was going to be impossible for Sue and me to pay for college for even one of them! "What's going to happen?" I fumed.

Now before I go on, I'd better say that my personal prayer life is likely to be quite informal, not only in the way I talk to God but also in the way I believe He answers. If we're supposed to be friends with God, I figure, why not talk that way?

In the silence that followed my monologue about the boys'

educations, I heard in my mind the Lord ask, *Can I handle that?*

I thought for several minutes. *Let's see*, I reminded myself, *He's all-powerful, He loves the boys, He's unlimitedly resourceful.* "All right, I guess You can handle my sons' educations."

Then I was off and running on other complaints. But at the end of each of them came the same question: *Can I handle that?* And after deliberation, I would reluctantly agree that He could. Finally, I could think of nothing that He couldn't handle about this illness and its ramifications. And I felt peaceful. Sort of. But then, without even thinking out what I was going to say, these words ripped off my lips: "What about my fear of pain?"

Immediately there came the reply, *Now we're at the heart of things, Mike. Can I handle that?* And I knew that we had indeed gotten to the heart of a big, big issue in my life.

I had long before reconciled myself to physical death. I even looked forward to it, knowing that I would then enter a quality of glory only dimly imaginable here on earth. But I had not reconciled myself to pain. I was, in fact, so frightened of pain that I avoided the very thought of it.

It was now about 4:30 A.M. There I sat, face to face with my enemy. Pain. And there was no escaping it this time. I shivered, both from the raw nighttime and from my fear.

Mike, I said to myself, *you've got cancer! You'd doggone well better deal with pain, starting right now!* I could feel my heart beating as I spoke. I could feel the clamminess of my hands and a cavernous emptiness in my stomach. I had watched parishioners die of cancer. I remembered their pain, and I shuddered. As I looked *my* pain in the face, I was beginning to say, "No way, there's just *no* way I could deal with—" when I recalled the question.

Can I handle that?

I noticed the emphasis on the word *that*, as though everything had been leading up to this final issue of pain.

Very often God answers my questions by way of Scripture. It darted through my mind that Peter could walk on water as long as he kept his attention on Jesus, but sank when he focused on himself or the waves.

With an effort, I took my eyes off the prospect of pain and put them onto God. Finally, against a desire not to believe it, I replied out loud,

"Yes. You can even handle my pain."

A peace settled over me, the first since I had stepped into the doctor's office that morning. He would escort me through any trials ahead. Lifting my hands upward, I praised Him and worshiped Him until about five. Then an irresistible tiredness swept over me and I went back to bed and slept soundly. Friday at the office I was no longer drowsy . . . in spite of my lack of sleep. All that long weekend I walked in peace and joy, no longer afraid of anything that would come my way.

Tuesday the phone rang at the office. Actually, I was unprepared for the news. "Everything's all right, Mike," the doctor said. "Your blood test was normal; you don't have cancer."

I slumped back in my chair, feeling that I had made a fool of myself over nothing. *Thank God I didn't tell anyone,* I thought.

But now there was the question, Was there some reason this scare came up in the first place?

A few days later the answer came in my prayer time. The whole episode was a part of God's caring, designed to flush out of the bushes my fear of pain. And why was it so important to expose that fear? *Because it was bigger to you than Me,* the Lord replied, and I had to admit that that had been true.

I don't want anything between you and Me, the Lord went on, *but your fear of pain was a wall between us and it blocked your view of Me, so I took steps to expose it.*

And this is how I walked through an experience that was uncomfortable for a while but that led to change. To growth. To freedom. To improved relationship with God. Any one of these results was a major victory. I found myself wondering if I had stumbled onto a pattern that I could use again. As I looked at the experience several assumptions began to emerge:

1. That God is personal and wants to communicate. Not just with mankind, but with me. That's no small assumption but without it nothing else would have followed.

2. That God knows me better than I know myself. I'd pushed down my fear of pain but that didn't change the fact of its presence.

3. That God wants me to be free and will lead me into adventures that will bring freedom.

4. That He doesn't care if these adventures are frightening, appear to wound, leave me defenseless. For Him the surgery experience is necessary to rid me of the malignancy of fear.

So far the initiative was altogether God's. But I sensed that there was an element that *I* had brought to the equation, too.

What was it? A certain cautious willingness to go along with what was happening *even though I didn't like it.*

That timid, feet-dragging *willingness* was just that, an act of my *will.* "All right, Lord, if You are love, then when I open myself up to You I open myself up to love. I'm willing to be. . . ." What? What was the word I was looking for? ". . . *vulnerable!*"

Vulnerable. That was it. To allow God to renew me in this

battle with the fear of pain, I had to let down my defenses. I had to be *vulnerable* to Him.

No sooner had I said the word to myself than I realized I didn't like the thought.

Vulnerability is an issue we seek to avoid in every place we might find it. Ask women, blacks, the uneducated and the homeless how much they like being vulnerable. We've had more than one hundred street people stay in our home over the years and not one of them relished his vulnerability to moneylessness, homelessness or to those of us who provided food and shelter for him. To go out in search of vulnerability is something most of us would not do. Just the opposite, we search for ways to become less vulnerable. You can spend hundreds of dollars in any well-stocked bookstore on material written to help you decrease your vulnerabilities, or at least conceal them until you can cover them more effectively. It is unquestioned that vulnerability is a bad thing, except among sophisticates playing bridge!

I became interested in the word itself and found that it comes from the Latin *vulner*, wound, thus, susceptible to injury, unprotected from danger. On a philosophical level, God, who is completely trustworthy, is not one from whom injury could be expected. My own experience, however, is that openness to God often *feels* and sometimes *seems* and may in fact *be* hazardous. The interactive nature of life with God requires that I be honest with Him where I think He has wounded me. That honesty is what gave Job such a tremendous encounter with God.

This business of interacting with God is the major priority in life. It's what this book is all about. The Church has produced many succinct statements about this—for example, the most well-known: "To enjoy God and be enjoyed by him forever," as the Westminster Catechism puts it. After that landmark experience with vulnerability in 1975 I became intrigued with the subject. It has been a key in my relationship with God that I have found too significant not to share.

Being vulnerable to God is a minute-by-minute process. He won't take our openness to Him as an invitation to change us overnight. A few years ago I read a book with the message "You must be broken." Well, I was eager for the things of God so I set out to be vulnerable to Him. In fact, I decided to *help* Him . . . and that was a mistake. Being vulnerable to God means letting Him take the initiative.

After I read about brokenness I went on a long mountain hike on which I decided to do something foolish that would embarrass me. *That* would "break" me, wouldn't it? I knelt to pray on a mountain trail, purposely forcing hikers to step over my feet as they passed. I was feeling extremely embarrassed and therefore "breaking" when one of the hikers asked as he stepped over me, "Hey, Bud, you looking for gold?" Then I felt just plain foolish. That should have ended my quest for brokenness, but it didn't.

Over the next few months I got it into my head that God wanted to break my pride. So I spent months trying to get up the courage to let God kill my pride. I was sure that He was the very hound of heaven hot on the heels of my pride, just waiting for that submissive moment when I might give Him the terminal nod. During a family vacation at Lake Tahoe, I decided to be over with it, walked to the edge of a clearing, grabbed hold of the bark of a Jeffrey pine tree and said, "All right, God, kill my pride." I waited. And waited. Nothing except confusion. Why hadn't He done it?

Two weeks later, back home in my quiet time, He answered me.

Because that would have decreased your need for Me. I was

stunned. My pride seemed to me to be a clear enemy. When I quieted down enough to hear Him again, He explained, *I created you for fellowship with Me, Mike. If I killed your pride all at once you'd go off and be humble on your own, without reference to Me. I will gladly give you humility on a moment-to-moment basis, but I would never kill your pride once and for all because then you wouldn't walk step by step with Me.*

That, of course, put my pride in an entirely new light. It was one of the most surprising and encouraging things that's ever been said to me.

Vulnerability to God means letting Him choose when and where He will set you free from your weaknesses. That's scary. We want to be healthy and holy right *now*. But we have to take the risk of letting Him decide.

This book attempts to look at some of the issues on which we might be confronted with vulnerability to God today. Some pertain to our private walk with God, some to our corporate walk, and are particularly appropriate in society and church today.

Before we proceed, however, there is a bit of background I need to share about the biblical view of humanity.

The Bible rarely categorizes anything neatly. And when we impose our own categories on the Bible we usually get into trouble. But occasionally the Bible does give parameters that help us understand its message. Paul provides us with such a structure when he says, "May your whole spirit, soul and body be kept blameless" (1 Thessalonians 5:23). On the next page is a diagram that helps us understand Paul's passage.

The body is the physical dimension of humanity (as opposed to its spiritual and soulish dimensions). The body begins at conception, grows, ages, dies and will be resurrected at the end of the age to live forever.

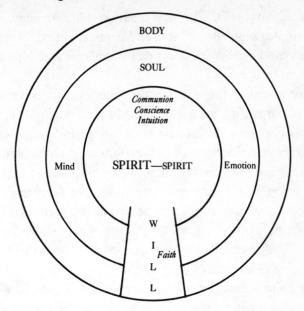

The soul is that part of our non-body that is distinctly human (as opposed to the spirit, which is in touch with the divine.) The soul's basic components are mind, emotions and will. These three factors combine in various ways to produce personality, intelligence, temperament, character, preference, fear, desire, skill and humor, to begin the list.

The spirit is that factor that is made "in the image of God" (Genesis 1:27; 5:1). The spirit is that part of us most like God, who "is Spirit" (John 4:24). We are born into the world with a dead spirit, which we inherited from our first father, Adam. As Paul put it, "In Adam all die" (1 Corinthians 15:22). The spirit comes alive by the operation of the will—by deciding that God's Son, Jesus, died and rose for our sins and is alive to enter our hearts if we invite Him to. When someone makes that invitation, the Holy Spirit brings the dead spirit to life, and melds Himself with it so that a new creation is formed

(2 Corinthians 5:17). This new creation is like an alloy. Brass, for example, is an alloy of zinc and copper, but when we look at brass candlesticks we don't call them zinc and copper; we call them brass.

Experientially, this means that when we perceive something in our spirits, we are perceiving it in the Spirit of God. On paper we can distinguish between an individual's spirit and the Holy Spirit by such expressions as "Spirit-spirit," but in experience they are the same. Over and over in this book we're going to run into the expression *The Lord said*. That denotes a communication that begins in the spirit and therefore begins in God, although it must be perceived in the mind. I'll say more about this when we talk about the word of knowledge in chapter 8.

The point is that the spirit is supposed to be in charge. To use a naval analogy, the body is the ship, the soul is a lieutenant and the spirit is the captain. In actual practice, however, the spirit is not in charge; the soul is because the soul harbors the mind. Since the "enlightenment" in Western civilization—from the late 1700s until today—the intellect has been in ascendancy. It now occupies a position of authority never intended by God. Today at last with the Holy Spirit movement in the Church we're relearning the use of our minds in submission to and under the inspiration of our spirits.

The will deserves special attention. The will is that part of us in touch with all the other parts. It is the faculty in which God has designed faith to work. Faith is not intellectual. It is not *anti*-intellectual but goes *beyond* the intellect. It operates in a sphere that is beyond the ability of the intellect to grasp. Nor is faith emotional. One need not *feel* faithful in order to *be* faithful. The will is capable of making decisions that are both irritating to our minds and uncomfortable to our emotions. Examples of this will occur frequently in these chapters.

I would like to suggest a prayer before we proceed: "Lord, let me see and get out of this book all that You want for me, and let me be blind to or gloss over what would be unhelpful for me."

Try to open your spirit to Him as you read, and see what happens.

2
Vulnerability to Scripture

In the summer of 1972 I experienced what is now almost tritely phrased a "life-changing spiritual renewal." I hadn't sought this experience—didn't even know that it was possible—but was deeply in need of it. One of the reasons I needed renewal so badly was that I had no anchor in my life.

Once I was renewed, I acquired an insatiable taste for reading the Bible and one day a thundering realization shook me, taking the form of this prayer: "Lord, to this point in my life I have criticized Your Word; from now on I'll let it criticize me."

I had, of course, been trained in seminary to "criticize" the Bible. I'm sure that the intent of my professors was not that I attack God's Word as an enemy, but that I bring intellectual and scholarly resources as lenses through which to examine it. But three years of this approach flavored my attitude—though I scarcely realized it—toward Scripture. By the time I had been in the ministry for several years, the Bible held no more real authority for me. If it was the "Word of God," I reasoned that there were also many other sources. And if I did not like something the Bible stated, I dismissed it as the no-longer-appropriate cultural bias of its human writers.

In addition to telling the Lord that I would no longer criticize His Word, I told Him that I would henceforth believe His Word until I was certain that it had let me down. Over the next few weeks, an eerie enlargement of my understanding began to occur. To describe this enlargement, let me use an analogy: If you think of the width of this page as representative of the spectrum of light, you'll have the ultraviolet end toward one edge, the infrared toward the other, and a space about half an inch wide in the center that represents visible light. Now simply translate the light spectrum as the spectrum of reality, with the half-inch in the middle representing the human intellect.

None of us has a mind capable of understanding the full spectrum of reality. Reality is infinite but our minds are finite. Before repenting of my criticism of the Bible, my problem had been that I refused credence to anything that I couldn't understand. It seems rather childish now, but my attitude was "If I can't understand it, it doesn't exist." Never mind that I didn't understand electricity at all but never doubted that it exists.

But then that sliver of understanding began to widen. I found I could understand things that had been mysteries to me before. Paul says, "The man without the Spirit does not accept the things that come from the Spirit of God, for they are foolishness to him, and he cannot understand them, because they are spiritually discerned" (1 Corinthians 2:14). That was a description of me!

I remember in seminary, for example, trying with all my might to understand what Jesus was saying to Nicodemus in John 3. One night I decided to crack this text open. I embanked myself with rows of commentaries, reading and rereading what they said. But I drew a complete blank on the phrase *born again*. I could identify with Nicodemus' confusion but not Jesus' certainty. Whatever could He have meant?

Finally, I pressed my forehead into the Bible, as though I could grasp it by osmosis. But I gave up, utterly frustrated, and certain that the Bible was unapproachable at significant points.

But now I saw it! My spirit had died when Adam had sinned. God had warned him: "Of the tree of the knowledge of good and evil you shall not eat, for *in the day* that you eat of it you shall die" (Genesis 2:17, RSV). What died in Adam when he disobeyed was his spirit, not his soul or body, although his body would eventually die as well. "As in Adam all die," Paul said. I could see that I had inherited a dead spirit. It wasn't that I deserved it or didn't deserve it; it was simply part of the package of being human. And I could see that to accept Jesus Messias willfully into my heart was to "be born of the Spirit."

What was the difference between my two experiences with the Bible, one in seminary and the second that had just occurred? In seminary I tried to understand Scripture with my intellect. Then . . . then I took that difficult step for a modern man and deliberately put aside my intellect. In other words I made myself vulnerable, ready to have my intellect wounded, which today is the same thing as having the center of our beings wounded.

What happened? Scripture was opened for me. Interestingly the experience was an enlargement of my understanding, a growth that did not come through academic attainment but through spiritual obtainment. Whereas before I had been blind to it, now I could see it clearly.

What's more, I now had a dawning awareness that there could be an anchor in this life, something that I could hitch myself to that would stand fast, no matter what winds were blowing. God Himself is, of course, that anchor. But He is Spirit-wind, which is not easily read. I need some things of

Him that I can *see,* and the best of these is His Word.[1] As we have seen in the diagram at the end of chapter 1, the will belongs to all three aspects of man—body, soul and spirit. I can give willful assent—the will of the spirit—to something the Bible says even though I do not fully (or even partially) understand it intellectually. That assent allows the reality of the Word to make an impact on my life. One of the usual impacts is understanding, eventually.

Part of being vulnerable to Scripture is to take it seriously enough to grapple with it, argue with it, agonize over it, let it make an impact on our lives. There is room for dialogue with God about what His Word means. Again, I tend to carry on this dialogue in a very informal way, as with a Father-friend. A wonderful example happened to me with John 15:5. I had been meditating through the Gospel of John for more than a year, when I ran up against "Apart from me you can do nothing."

"Come on, Lord," I exclaimed. "I've done all kinds of things without You."

Name one, came the reply.

"One? I could name hundreds."

One will do.

By now it was dawning on me that He might have a different definition of "thing" than mine. I knew that I had done all manner of *wrong* things without Him, which, presumably, were excluded from the argument at hand. Well, even if He meant *good* things, I was sure I had done some of those also without His involvement. Thinking to end the argument swiftly, I mentioned one glorious weekend some years before when I had led a planning group to a wonderful conclusion.

---

[1] Sacraments are also good physicalizers of God's love—seeable, tasteable, touchable objects that are imbued with and speak to us reassuringly of God's grace toward us.

Instantly God gave me a threefold revelation. The first was that good did indeed happen on that weekend; the second was that it happened *in spite of* me, not because of me; and the third was that the good was attributable to a mousy fellow who didn't talk much but had been praying the whole weekend. That knocked me down, but I refused to be counted out, yet.

So over the next few months, I put "goods" I had done on a list: things I had done without reference to God. Many items came off the list when put under scrutiny, but eventually I had five things that were unassailably good and that I had done without so much as a thought toward God.

Rubbing my hands together in expectancy of victory, I said to the Lord one day, "Well, I'm ready to go up against You on John 15:5 again."

Come, He replied.

"All right. What about the time I . . . ." and I named one of my five "goods."

Instantly came the revelation again. The thing I had done had not been a good at all! I had been self-deceived. It's difficult to express the impact of this experience. Nothing in me could argue with the revelation. I was embarrassed that I hadn't seen the self-deception myself. How could I ever have thought that thing was good?

But like a man trying to ignore that his boat is sinking, I plunged on to item two. It was brutally crushed. Item three: demolished. Item four: massacred. Finally, I had no stomach for this game, grabbed the arms of the chair for stability and exclaimed, "What the hell is going on?" (I didn't mean to be profane, just emphatic.) Instead of stability, I got more revelation, though my mind was already reeling. Into my mind's eye came the image of a ruler five inches long.

Came a voice, *Maybe if you mobilized all your natural abilities, you could produce this much good.* About an inch was measured off. Not much! *And a better man than you might do this much.*

About four inches were measured off. Humbling it was, I tell you.

Then the five-inch ruler was whisked off, stage left, and replaced with one from the right that read in the millions of inches at eye level. It seemed to reach from the center of the earth up to heaven. And the voice, a touch slyly, said, *If you acknowledge that without Me you can do nothing, I'll give you* My *value scale*, and there it was before my eyes. Now I'm rebellious, doltish, brutish and bad, but I'm not stupid, so I recognized this as a good deal.

"You're on!" I replied aloud, and the episode quickly faded to a close.

Over the next six weeks I began noticing an internal something I couldn't put my finger on, but that couldn't be dismissed. I would try to examine it periodically, but it eluded my understanding. Yet it continued to grow. One morning, during my prayer time, it came out of its hiding place and was revealed. *My lifelong inferiority complex had simply evaporated.* As soon as I recognized it, I erupted into thirty minutes of praise. This was deliverance! This was an almost unhoped-for blessing. This was—wait a minute! *Why* did this happen? I wasn't even working on my inferiorities. Why should they have simply evaporated?

A five-inch ruler came to mind, then a million-inch ruler, then the words *I'll give you* My *value*.

I said, flabbergasted, "You mean to tell me that my inferiority complex has disappeared because I acknowledged that I could do nothing without You?"

Yes.

And I went into another half hour of praise. What a glorious, unforeseen gift of grace! I didn't comprehend much of it, but I had the emotional proof that I was no longer suffering under inferiority. My soul shouted, "Hallelujah!" God was lending me His immeasurable value. I had the promise of His presence whenever I put my hand to a task in His name. I never thought it would be so much fun to be so rich . . . because I was impoverished. Later, as always, came living words to explain it.

"Blessed are the poor in spirit, for theirs is the kingdom of heaven" (Matthew 5:3). I paraphrased it, "Blessed are you, Mike, if you know you're spiritually impoverished, for I can entrust the Kingdom to folks like that."[2]

"Whoever loses his life for my sake will find it" (Matthew 10:39). I had agreed to the loss of my natural abilities and gained the promise of God's abilities in their places.

"I praise you, Father, Lord of heaven and earth, because you have hidden these things from the wise and learned, and revealed them to little children" (Luke 10:21). From every direction came the confirmation that something wonderfully topsy-turvy was occurring.

When this experience was over I knew that it would not have occurred without vulnerability to Scripture. The Word itself says that it is fully alive (Hebrews 4:12). It is an incredible opportunity to dialogue with something as wonderfully alive and pertinent and wise as the Scriptures.

When should you agree readily with what you do not understand and when should you fight with it? I don't know. But I do know that our fighting with it must be like Jacob wrestling with the angel until he got blessed. Somehow we must fight with Scripture in the hope of losing, for loss is the gateway to gain.

A favorite slogan of mine is "It took the Holy Spirit to *write* Scripture and it takes the Holy Spirit to *read* Scripture." I

---

[2] "Poor" in Greek is *ptochoi*, which describes the cower of a beggar and means "powerless to enrich."

think that conservatives and liberals alike make a big mistake if they approach the Scriptures without benefit of the Spirit. A wooden literalism and a cavalier agnosticism alike deaden that which claims for itself that it is "living and active. Sharper than any double-edged sword, it penetrates even to dividing soul and spirit." Most of us would claim, I suppose, that we seek God's input when reading the Bible, but my hunch is that it really isn't so. The mistakes seem to run along these lines: legalism about the Word hinders conservatives and resisting its piercing hinders liberals.

Let me ask a question: Do you examine the Scriptures or do they examine you? You do both, of course, but if the emphasis is on the former, then *you* are the judge and you are likely only to learn what *you* are capable of discerning. But if the emphasis is on the latter, then the Bible is the judge and you are likely to learn a good deal more because you have the discernment of the minds that produced the Scriptures and the Mind that activated them. Each morning I sit down to read the Bible with this prayer on my lips: "Lord, open Your Word to me and open me to Your Word." The second phrase is the more crucial. Like no other book, the Bible is more open to those of a humble rather than a proud approach. As Goethe said, "I read all kinds of books, including sacred books, but the Bible stands alone because it reads me."

Jesus on Scripture: The Law

To be vulnerable to Scripture, then, is to be subject to its "reading" of you. I was particularly interested in seeing how Jesus regarded Scripture. He is my Lord, after all, and I seek to follow Him, so I needed to get His attitudes toward Scripture. I skimmed through the Gospels looking for His references to the Bible—which in His day was the Old Testament.

Those few hours were startling. I counted 47 direct quotes or specific references that Jesus made to the Old Testament.

In the temptation account in Matthew 4, Jesus' response to Satan was to quote Scripture at him. It seemed sufficient to Jesus simply to announce pertinent passages from Deuteronomy 6 and 8 in response to the temptations. After the third temptation, Jesus added His own comment, "Away from me, Satan! For it is written. . . ." That's all! The tactic was effective, for the end of the matter is, "Then Satan left him."

It would seem in this episode that Jesus regarded Scripture as the final authority by which to squelch Satan's evil intentions. And Satan agreed, apparently, for he did not contest Jesus' use of Scripture. He *did* try to manipulate Jesus by his own judicious quoting of Scripture, but Jesus remained unmanipulated, exercising discrimination regarding the right and wrong use of God's Word.

In Matthew 5, Jesus showed that He was no mindless babbler of Scripture. Rather He demonstrated a remarkable ability to plumb to its originally intended applications in His formula, "You have heard that it was said to the people long ago. . . . But *I* tell you . . ." (verses 21–22).

Throughout His ministry it was apparent that Jesus had spent much time studying and meditating on Scripture. He could say with great force, "Do not think that I have come to abolish the Law or the Prophets; I have not come to abolish them but to fulfill them" (verse 17). He went on to say, "I tell you the truth, until heaven and earth disappear, not the smallest letter, not the least stroke of a pen, will by any means disappear from the Law until everything is accomplished" (verse 18).

This is a powerful statement on the veracity of Scripture. What's more, He concluded this comment with a warning: "Anyone who breaks one of the least of these commandments and teaches others to do the same will be called least in the kingdom of heaven, but whoever practices and teaches these commands will be called great in the kingdom of heaven" (verse 19).

But on another occasion He threw out whole sections of Old Testament dietary laws when He said, "Listen to me, everyone, and understand this. Nothing outside a man can make him 'unclean' by going into him. Rather, it is what comes out of a man that makes him 'unclean' " (Mark 7:14).[3] The disciples were apparently astonished at this comment, for they asked Him about it immediately in private. Jesus' reply was to repeat what He had said in public, to which Mark adds, "In saying this, Jesus declared all foods 'clean' " (verse 19).

I think it is important to recognize that Jesus regarded the Law in a procedural mindset—copied later by the apostle Paul: "We have been released from the law so that we serve in the new way of the Spirit" (Romans 7:6). The Law served a purpose that was superseded by Jesus Christ who saves man from the Law's just condemnation.

Also, the Law is a clumsy director of human behavior. At best, it can only point in the general direction of right behavior—for example: "Do not commit adultery." But Jesus reinterpreted the Law, translating it from an exterior influence to an internalized matter of the heart: "Look not with lust at another woman." A man can obey the letter of the former while demolishing the intent of the latter. About this particular matter it has always helped me to ask myself, "As I look at women, do I have *taking* eyes or *giving* eyes?" If I am

[3] While we're talking about attitudes toward Scripture in this section, let's not miss the point of Jesus' teaching here: It is not the presence in us of tendencies toward sin that defiles us. Rather it is the coming forth of these things, the expression of them, that defiles us. Sinning is behavioral, not existential.

trying to take pleasure from them as I gaze at them, I am in
danger of irritating the conscience of Jesus, but if I am trying
to give blessing to them, then Jesus' spirit soars.

Jesus on Scripture: Prophecy

If Jesus' vulnerability to the Law was complex, not so with
messianic prophecy. Jesus' comments and actions in reference
to predictions about Himself were simple and clear. I can find
no place in the Bible where Jesus challenged messianic prophecy. On several occasions He took pains to fulfill these predictions, never questioning their propriety, possibility or cost.

Consider the triumphal entry into Jerusalem. Zechariah had
predicted: "Rejoice greatly, O Daughter of Zion! Shout,
Daughter of Jerusalem! See, your king comes to you, righteous and having salvation, gentle and riding on a donkey, on
a colt, the foal of a donkey" (Zechariah 9:9). If getting into
town was His objective, He could have done it a lot more
simply. But the Scriptures had foretold that He would get into
town *that* way, so He did it that way. Notice that the fulfillment of this prophecy took the collaboration of many others;
the owner of the donkey and colt had to release them and the
populace had to gather in significant numbers and erupt spontaneously into praise. I detect the hand of God in these details.

Psalm 41:9 had predicted, "Even my close friend, whom I
trusted, he who shared my bread, has lifted up his heel against
me." Remember how Jesus said, "The one who has dipped
his hand into the bowl with me will betray me" (Matthew
26:23)? And remember in John, "As soon as Judas took the
bread, Satan entered into him. 'What you are about to do, do
quickly,' Jesus told him" (13:27)? Jesus may even be said to
have participated in Judas' betrayal, not trying to dissuade

him but, in fact, facilitating the speed with which he did it, and making sure that he had that prophesied piece of bread in his hand before he went.

If ever a man had a right to defend himself during a court trial, it was Jesus. But prophecy said that "as a sheep before her shearers is silent, so he did not open his mouth" (Isaiah 53:7). So "the high priest stood up and said to Jesus, 'Are you not going to answer? What is this testimony that these men are bringing against you?' But Jesus remained silent" (Matthew 26:62). Jesus would only tell who He was; He would not answer charges. (Good advice for many who are under persecution.)

In addition to Jesus' deliberate fulfillment of messianic prophecies, the Father Himself saw to it that others—beyond Jesus' control—were satisfied also. At one point Jesus quoted Zechariah 13:7 as proof that His disciples would fall away and abandon Him (Matthew 26:31). The Scriptures said it would happen, therefore it would happen. And it did. (There are too many to document in this text. I refer you to the footnote to see several items and their prophetic and fulfillment references.[4])

---

[4] That Jesus would be the "offspring of a woman"—Genesis 3:15, Galatians 4:4.

That He would be born in Bethlehem—Micah 5:2, Matthew 2:1.

Of a virgin—Isaiah 7:14, Matthew 1:18.

The escape into Egypt—Hosea 11:1, Matthew 2:14.

His ministry in Galilee—Isaiah 9:1–2, Matthew 4:12–16.

His rejection by His own people—Isaiah 53:3, John 1:11.

That He would be sold for thirty pieces of silver—Zechariah 11:12, Matthew 26:15.

That the money paid for Him would buy the potter's field—Zechariah 11:13, Matthew 27:6–7.

That He would be crucified with sinners—Isaiah 53:12, Matthew 27:38.

That His hands and feet would be pierced—Psalm 22:16, John 20:27.

That He would be given gall and vinegar—Psalm 69:21, John 19:29.

That His side would be pierced—Zechariah 12:10, John 19:34.

(Continued on next page)

There is an interesting passage in 1 Samuel 3:19, "The Lord was with Samuel as he grew up, and he let none of his words fall to the ground." Once in a while I picture Jesus sitting up in heaven with the Father before the Incarnation and hearing some prophet say something about Him, only to exclaim to the Father, "Why did You let him say *that?*", knowing that He would have to fulfill it. My point is that Jesus was radically obedient—vulnerable—to prophecy.

Jesus and the Scriptures: Miracles

Vulnerability is openness. Vulnerability is being willing to take risks. Nowhere would this be more evident than with miracles. Jesus was totally open to miracles, an attitude that is difficult for us to understand today.

My tendency, for example, used to be to ask, "But *how* did these things occur?" If I could not grasp the *how* I would not allow the *what*. Interestingly, God did nothing to answer my questions. But once I began to allow the what, I began to see the how, because it happened in my own life. Early on in my days of renewal, for instance, a man named Martin, with a severe back problem, contacted me. He had been hit on the job by a backhoe, which had put him into traction for months. The doctors wanted to operate on his spine to alleviate his pain, but Martin wanted to try prayer first.

Well, I didn't much want to pray for him, fearing that nothing would occur and he would be all the more discouraged and I would look like a fool, etc. (You know the drill.) But, well,

That soldiers would gamble for His clothes—Psalm 22:18, Mark 15:24.
That no bone would be broken—Psalm 34:20, John 19:33.
That He would be buried in a tomb of the rich—Isaiah 53:9, Matthew 27:57–60.
That He would be resurrected—Psalm 16:10, Matthew 28:9.
That He would ascend to heaven—Psalm 68:18, Luke 24:50–51.

he asked, and I couldn't think of a nice-sounding reason to decline, so I went to his home. He could get out of traction a few hours each day and was sitting in a walker-chair when I arrived. We chatted a bit about his problem and I made a decision to get it over quickly, so I said, "Well, Martin, let's pray."

The lower part of the backrest was open, so I placed my hand on the small of his back and began to pray. In a few seconds I noticed that his back was shifting under my hand. I was new to this kind of thing and didn't know what to do, but I kept on praying that God would realign his back and heal it. After a couple minutes of this, I couldn't contain my curiosity any longer, asking, "Martin, are you making your back do that?"

"No," he replied, amazed, adding, "and I feel a lot of heat."

"Let's pray some more," I replied, with a feeling that this strange thing might stop if we talked too long.

The upshot was that he went back onto the job a few weeks later with his doctors' permission, completely healed.

I still don't know *how* God healed him but I do know *that* He healed him. And the embarrassment of not knowing how is a cheap price to pay for the what. Deciding to believe that healings in the Bible were actually true has been one of the factors that has freed them to occur in my life.

Finally, there is an intriguing exchange between Jesus and the Sadducees in Matthew 22:23–33. A seemingly clever trap has been set by His opponents, to which Jesus responds with a stinging rebuke as well as an example of His own interpretation of Scripture.

"You are in error because you do not know the Scriptures or the power of God." That's the rebuke.

"But about the resurrection of the dead—have you not read

what God said to you, 'I am the God of Abraham, the God of Isaac, and the God of Jacob'? He is not the God of the dead but of the living." That's the interpretation.

The rebuke is that they do not know Scripture. The interpretation turns on the tense of a verb. "I am [not "I was"] the God of people who have died; therefore, they are still alive; therefore, there is resurrection from the dead." So goes Jesus' argument. That's a fairly close reading of Scripture, isn't it? You could almost say, in this passage at least, that Jesus is a literalist.

I think Jesus' rebuke of the Sadducees could be aimed at much of the Church today. We don't *know* the Scriptures or the power of God, in the sense of being intimate with the Word. I cannot experience the fullness of intimacy with my wife if I stand in doubt of her. Nor can I experience the power of God if I stand in doubt of His testimony about it.

Does this mean that we have to throw away two hundred years of Western thought in order to relate with the God of the Bible? My response to that question launches us into the next two chapters.

3
Vulnerability to Discomfort

In October 1984 I was on the team that went with John Wimber—the founder of Vineyard Ministries International—to London to participate in a Power Ministry Conference. During one of his talks John said, "We are never comfortable. We never know if God is going to heal someone, if the Kingdom will be expanded, if the people will be discipled. But we go on anyway."

I had gone to London to learn how to heal the sick. I knew the basic procedure[1] but lacked experience, which I hoped the conference was to supply. It sure did. I was getting experience morning, noon and night. But as I heard John say, "We are never comfortable," I realized that comfort had been my unconscious goal. I had assumed that once I had enough experience, I would attain comfort in ministering to the sick.

What's more, comfort loomed in the basement of my soul as the foundation upon which effectiveness would rest. It was an

---

[1] The "Five-Step Healing Process," as it has come to be called, is an excellent model for ministering to the sick. It is honest, is learnable by great numbers of people, has personal, sociological and theological integrity, and it works. The last two chapters of Wimber's book *Power Healing* fully describe this process.

unexamined assumption that once I was comfortable I would be effective. As John's talk went on, I tuned out. As I contemplated these new thoughts about comfort, I began to realize that it had attained the status of being almost an idol in my life.

Material Comfort

I had simply assumed that I had to be safely fitted out with a house, car, clothes, food, office, desk, secretary and enough books and money before I could be expected to produce effective ministry. Comfortableness in these *things* was the foundation for my ministry. Once it is baldly stated like that, it is absurd, of course. But I had not noticed the absurdity until it was stated.

Preparation Comfort

Someone once said, "In the space of three years, Jesus of Nazareth fed thousands, healed hundreds and trained twelve." That is a marvelous distillation of what ministry is all about. I believe that the Lord is challenging ministers— ordained and lay—to train others, following the model of their Model. I could say a great deal more about that, having led about fifteen clergy conferences on leadership development in the last few years.

We can, however, easily become idolatrous of preparation. I have observed this at work particularly when we demand more preparation than a given task requires. You don't have to possess a degree in theology in order to tell someone about Jesus. You don't have to have a total inner healing before you can listen effectively to someone else who has problems. There has grown up in our culture an expectation that you must be equipped to handle whatever might possibly occur before you put your hand to any task. What we are afraid of is the Peter Principle, wherein we rise to the level of our incompetence. Hey, what's wrong with saying, "Now we have gotten out of my league"? Even Jesus refused to deal with some situations that came His way, saying with one refusal, "Who made *Me* a judge over you?" (see Luke 12:14).

God never asks us to do something that He won't enable us to do. I remember taking in our first stranger. A social worker came to my office to ask if my family would take a homeless teenage boy to live with us for a while. As my wife and I discussed it we wondered: What if he is on drugs and influences our sons negatively? What if he steals the silver? What if he is unbalanced and tries to harm one of us? How long might this be for?

All of these were worthy considerations. But we kept remembering, "I was a stranger and you invited Me in" (Matthew 25:35). We decided to go for it. And that young man lived with us for more than a year. Were there problems? Yes. Did they overwhelm us? Absolutely not. We had no experience in taking in strangers, we barely knew the Lord, we knew nothing of how to pray for protection and had little training in dealing with disturbed people. But God taught us all these things as we went along.

Abraham's servant, telling how he had successfully obtained a wife for Isaac, said, "I *being in the way*, the Lord led me" (Genesis 24:27, KJV). If we are on the Lord's path, He will lead us, too.

It is true that sometimes life presents us with challenges that are clearly beyond our ability. Do we then just bow out? Look at that odd behavior of Jesus toward the barren fig tree. You remember that Jesus was staying in Bethany, just a couple of miles from Jerusalem.

> The next day as they were leaving Bethany, Jesus was
> hungry. Seeing in the distance a fig tree in leaf, he went

to find out if it had any fruit. When he reached it, he found nothing but leaves, *because it was not the season for figs*. Then he said to the tree, "May no one ever eat fruit from you again." And his disciples heard him say it. . . . In the morning, as they went along, they saw the fig tree withered from the roots.

Mark 11:12–14, 20

As you can see from the italicized phrase, it was unrealistic of Jesus to expect figs on that tree. Yet He expected figs anyway. Why? And what is the point?

Why? Because He had a need and made a demand on part of His creation to fill that need. What's the point? You can bear fruit out of season if it is the Lord who tells you to. The King of creation feels He has the liberty to make unseasonal demands on us and that we will respond with faith and obedience to those demands. He demonstrated this fact on a fig tree, but the point is clearly for persons.

At the heart of being willing to embrace discomfort is a determination not to compete with God. God is the agent of creation, not you or me. Much avoidance of discomfort is spawned by a desire not to need Him. We don't want to be dependent on God; we want to be competent or useful of ourselves. It is all for His glory, of course, but just let me marshall my natural gifts and present the fruit of my hands to Him. Don't make me dependent on Him. Not yet. I'm not ready.

Fear: The Enemy of Ministry

In the early days of the Salvation Army, a big man used to go with the young women to preach on street corners. He wore a sandwich board sign that proclaimed *Delivered from fear of public opinion*. This fellow had won a victory over fear!

Fear is one of the greatest discomforts we must be willing to face in order to be effective. About five years ago I scheduled a seminar at St. Jude's called "A Day of Healing." After teaching on physical healing it came time to put the teaching to work. I asked if anyone had an ailment that, if God healed it, would be immediately evident. A woman came up who had one leg shorter than the other, causing her considerable back pain.

Fear invaded my thoughts: What if it worked? I had heard "leg-lengtheners" mentioned with great ridicule and doubt, and I did not want to be the target of such ridicule. But here was this lady before me. So I helped her to a chair, making sure her backside was firmly against it and that her legs were straight and that her shoes were firmly on her feet. As I took her feet in my hands, sure enough, the left leg was about half an inch shorter than the right. Just as I was about to pray, another pang of fear seized me: What if it *didn't* work? I would look the fool if I told that leg to grow out and nothing happened! But I was committed, so, in spite of my fear, I told the leg to grow out. And you know what? It did! In three seconds that heel was exactly level with the other. And she exclaimed, "Oh! I felt my leg shift!"

Another example. Later we had a day-long seminar on what at that point was a new area for me, "Calling Down the Holy Spirit." After I had taught for a while, it was time to ask the Holy Spirit to make Himself manifest. I prayed that ludicrously inadequate-feeling prayer, "Come, Holy Spirit," and waited to see what would happen. After about sixty seconds I couldn't see that anything had happened, and I began to feel panicky. Straining to have faith, I was telling the Spirit, "You'd better show up. I insist that You show up!" But nothing was happening. I searched people's faces desperately for some sign of His presence.

People were starting to get restless, some had opened their eyes, disappointment was spreading. I had to act. I couldn't wait any longer. Yet no one was manifesting His presence the way I had seen in Wimber's meetings. Just when defeat seemed inevitable, I noticed that one woman looked incrementally more peaceful than when we had begun. So I approached her, put my hand on her shoulder, and said, "Thank You, Holy Spirit, that You're resting on Heather. I bless what You're doing in her." Immediately the peace deepened in her into a kind of holy joy. Within two minutes, people all over the room were manifesting the Spirit's presence. And there followed ninety minutes of rich, effective ministry that touched almost every person there.

In these examples, fear was a major threat. It tried to sabotage what the Lord wanted to do. Let's spend a few minutes looking at three sources of fear and possible answers to them.

Fear #1: Not Wanting to Be Made a Fool

Nobody with an intact ego relishes the opportunity to botch up a ministry situation. But if we are to grow in usefulness, we will always need to have a growing edge: an area of ministry in which we haven't enough experience or insight or confidence. Fear rises up and motivates us to take the safe path. But the safe path may have a high price: no growth for us and less help for the one being ministered to.

I think the best answer to the fear of looking foolish is to have a firm grasp on the basis of our acceptability. In its shortest form, this basis follows these steps:

1. *You feel you are not acceptable.* You really are, but probably don't believe it, so let's start where you are.
2. *God accepts you anyway.* He sees you "in Christ." What is

true of Christ is true of you, in His eyes. It is a status that He *gives* you, not because you deserve it, but because Jesus deserves it.

3. *You can accept God's acceptance of you.* He created you with a capacity to receive that acceptance. It is an act of the will.

4. *His acceptance makes you acceptable.* It transforms you, again, in His eyes. You can decide to agree with Him that you are acceptable and accepted because of what God has done for you in Christ Jesus.

5. *Now you can accept yourself in Christ.* If you want to be someone, on your own, apart from Christ, then I haven't much encouragement for you. But if you don't mind being accepted *in Christ*, then I have all encouragement for you. Whatever the Father thinks of the Son, He thinks of you. Whatever the Father feels for the Son, He feels for you. And He challenges you to think His opinions of yourself and feel His feelings for you, and thus complete what He has done for you.[2]

People who discover Jesus as the basis of their acceptability have wonderful latitude to try their hands at all kinds of things. If you flub it, you are still *acceptable*.

Fear #2: Not Wanting to Hurt Anyone

We do not want to mislead, falsely encourage or improperly minister to people. But fear often immobilizes ministry, too.

Understanding the nature of faith is a great help here in overcoming this fear. Francis MacNutt asked a man who had studied the Gospel of Mark for 25 years how a first-century Jew would have regarded faith. *"Chutzpah!"* he answered. Nerve. Now to a nice, middle-class, responsible Christian,

[2] If you have been dealt a number of hurts in your life, you may need inner healing before you allow yourself to experience the fullness of the Father's opinions and feelings for you. See pages 152*ff* for a simple model by which to do inner healing for yourself and others.

the word *nerve* is too nervy to be relied upon as the normal ingredient for working with God. But that's how it is. God Himself has authored this reckless manner of getting His things done. "Without faith it is impossible to please God" (Hebrews 11:6). I am convinced that nothing significant in the Kingdom happens without the expenditure of nerve. It takes *chutzpah* to pray for a healing when to do so may not result in immediate relief. The person prayed for will certainly be disappointed, perhaps even hurt. A friend of mine once lamented to John Wimber, "I need more faith." John replied, "Not really. What you need is more courage."

Here is where the will comes into play again. Courage is not being unafraid; it is feeling afraid and willfully—faithfully— taking action anyway.

If you make it your primary intent to love people, that will come through. If you have communicated love, then people have already been ministered to, even if your prayers seem to fail. And if you love yourself, you will be less inclined to make dumb claims beforehand about what God is or is not going to do. You rarely *know* that God is going to do a specific thing; it is enough to trust Him and proceed with the attitude "Let's pray and see what God does." That does not overcommit you or Him or the one receiving prayer.

Fear #3: Not Being Sure of Your Guidance

Jesus made an astonishing statement about how He worked. He said, "The Son can do nothing by himself; he can do only what he sees his Father doing" (John 5:19). This theme is restated in the Gospel of John at least fifteen times. And He made the same statement about us: "Apart from me you can do nothing" (John 15:5), about which I have testified earlier. Jesus was helpless on His own; we are helpless on our own.

For Him and for us that means a coming to terms with discomfort. For Him and for us that means using the word of knowledge, because it is a pivotal gift. *We must be able to see what He is doing in order to be fruitfully occupied.*

There is a whole chapter on guidance in this book, a section of which will deal with the word of knowledge. My point for the moment is that God speaks in a "whis," which is half a whisper. I do dearly wish that He would speak in a roar, but He rarely does. He expects us to take action on what seems woefully insufficient guidance. We want "to be sure." Sureness seems a responsible requirement to us. But requiring that we be sure is making an end-run around Hebrews 11:6, which clearly places *faith*, not sureness, as the indispensable factor in pleasing God.

The answer to wanting to be sure is to accept discomfort.

Discomfort is never finished. You do not scrape up your courage and take a risk, hoping never to have to do it again. Instead, you take a risk only to find that another—and perhaps greater—risk awaits you at the very next point of collaboration with God.

The other day I counted up how many conferences I have led in the last five years. The total came to 74 events in which 305 sessions occurred. In every one of those sessions the time of teaching was followed by my or a team member's saying, "Come, Holy Spirit." Every one of those 305 times I felt a stab of fear. "What if nothing happens?" "What if He comes and I don't know what to do?"

But you know what? I don't mind the discomfort anymore. I have learned to accept the risk/reward equation as working in my favor. Hundreds of people have been taught, healed, delivered, anointed and discipled at the price of discomfort. What maximal payoff at minimal cost! Further, once you are reconciled with discomfort, once you accept its presence as a normative, then it loses much of its bluster.

There are many kinds of discomforts other than those I have mentioned here. To jump-start your recognition of your own, I offer:

A Selected List of Discomforts

1. *Having to confess to someone you have offended.* This must rank right up there with the most difficult. Years ago when I was a brash young vicar, I fell out with a woman who had run our altar guild for decades. She stopped coming to church, but I justified myself that she should make the first move because I was "in the right." Three times the Lord told me to go to her house and ask her forgiveness. The last time I was driving on the freeway, just minutes from her exit. There was an emphasis in the Lord's message: This was the last time He would tell me. If I thought about it I knew I would chicken out, so I took her exit quickly and in another minute was walking up to her porch.

I knocked, praying that she wouldn't be home. Foolish prayer. In seconds the door opened and I asked if I could come in. Graciously she assented. Sitting down, I decided to get it over quickly, so I apologized for any hurt I had caused her in our disagreement and asked for her forgiveness, which she quickly gave. So quickly, in fact, that I sensed she, too, had been feeling disturbed over the ruptured relationship. Probably the Lord had asked me to accept discomfort not for my sake but for hers. A few months later she contracted a virulent form of pneumonia and died within a week. I was so grateful that the Lord had arranged our reconciliation in time.

2. *Having your ideas rejected.* I spend a lot of time trying to hear what God is saying about the direction He wishes to take

our congregation. Sometimes my ideas are shot to pieces by the staff. And sometimes someone comes into my office with a "really good idea" that *I* reject. How we respond to those who reject our ideas is a measure of our maturity. Do we flounce out, nurse our wounds and look for someone more compatible with us? Or do we go "back to the drawing board" in humility, ask for discernment and be ready to incorporate the other's suggestions, believing that God is working through him or her as well as through us?

3. *Hearing complaints about you.* Each of us suffers from poisons in our personalities, blips in our behaviors. When the feedback comes—as it most surely will—how do we respond? Paul, in a similar situation, prayed like mad for opposition to his leadership to be "taken away." But the opposition didn't budge. So he decided to listen to God on the subject, only to hear, "When you are weak, I am strong." Was he going to seek God's reputation or his own? Paul's answer proves to me that he really had a heart for God, for he exclaimed, "Therefore I will boast all the more gladly about my weaknesses" (see 2 Corinthians 10–12, especially 12:7–10).

4. *Giving away your ministry/prerogatives/privileges.* One day about five and a half years ago, through another pastor, the Lord said, *Give away the counseling ministry.* Counseling was about 65 percent of my professional self-image. I had taken many courses, read many books and seen many counselees in order to develop that ministry. Now He was saying give it up? The trouble was that I sensed the other pastor was really hearing from God. I felt confused, unappreciated and worried about how I would justify my salary if I agreed. When I asked, "Why?" God was silent. Finally, after three days, I said, "Oh, all right!" and began transferring my counseling load to lay-persons in our church. Much to my astonishment, I found that they exercised this ministry with greater results than I had.

When I asked Him about it, I felt the Lord told me, *I anointed them for that ministry; I never anointed you for it.* I think that is a devastating commentary on the assumption in our churches that if you are called to counseling you have to become ordained.

After a while, the Lord opened up the conference ministry I noted earlier. I never could have done it if I had still been counseling.

Since then, I have challenged a number of my lay leaders to ask God if they should give away *their* ministries to others in the church. They could hear me say that because they had seen me do it. The result is that there are now lots of people in our congregation who can effectively minister to a wide range of needs.

This is an imperfect world. That's O.K. because this is also a temporary world. Think of it this way: If eternity were, say, a million years long and the average life span seventy, then eternity would be 14,285 times longer than a lifetime here on earth. One minute here would be worth eleven *days* there. Now I ask you: Doesn't it seem reasonable to put up with a lifetime of discomfort here in order to collaborate in the incalculable glory that our obedience will permit the Lord to achieve for eternity?

4
Vulnerability to Jesus' Worldview

Imagine this: An American woman has walked into a clothes shop in the Arab quarter of old Jerusalem. She barely acknowledges the shopkeeper when she enters, going directly to a rack on which hang some garments. The shopkeeper makes several attempts at small talk, which she ignores. Holding a garment against her, she decides to purchase it, asking the price. Immediately she pays the asked-for price, receives the parcel and walks out. The shopkeeper spits on the street behind her retreating feet. He is obviously anti-American, right?

But wait a moment. Another American woman enters just a moment later. The shopkeeper greets her and she turns her full gaze on him and engages in several moments' conversation. Then she looks at the items in his shop and she, too, decides to make a purchase. He states the price. She bargains with him and in a few moments they agree on a price. As she receives the parcel and leaves the store, the shopkeeper smiles pleasantly.

What made the difference in the attitude of the shopkeeper toward the two women? It had to do with the worldviews of the women and the shopkeeper, the specifics of which we will review later in this chapter. What is a worldview?

Definitions of Worldview

James Sire gives us the simplest statement in *The Universe Next Door:* "A worldview is a set of presuppositions (or assumptions) which we hold (consciously or unconsciously) about the basic makeup of our world."

Dr. Paul Hiebert states it this way: "At the center of a culture is its 'worldview'—the fundamental way it organizes and perceives the world. . . . This 'core' is made up of:

1. Existential assumptions about what exists and how it is organized.
2. Affective assumptions about the nature of feelings.
3. Normative assumptions about the nature of values, priorities, and allegiances."[1]

Finally, Charles Kraft wraps up the idea in this fashion:

> Cultures pattern perceptions of reality into conceptualizations of what reality can or should be, what is to be regarded as actual, probable, possible, and impossible. These conceptualizations form what is termed the "worldview" of the culture. The worldview is the central systematization of conceptions of reality to which the members of the culture assent (largely unconsciously) and from which stems their value system. The worldview lies at the very heart of the culture, touching, interfacing with, and strongly influencing every aspect of culture.[2]

What these scholars are describing is a filtering system by which people both see and interpret their world.

[1] This material from lecture notes is used with Dr. Hiebert's permission.
[2] *Christianity and Culture* (Maryknoll, N.Y.: Orbis Books, 1979), p. 60.

How It Works Personally

All of us have run into people of our own ethnic origin who have a different viewpoint from our own. They might seem to be matters of temperament or taste. But, actually, they are worldview differences, according to the definitions given above. Even though people of the same ethnic origin have similar cultural worldviews, their personal worldviews can vary greatly.

Now this has a lot to do with vulnerability because it is when we are open to—vulnerable to—another's personal worldview that real communication can begin to take place. Years ago our first son, Kevin, and my wife, Sue, were having a difficult time of it. The relationship was saved thanks to a psychological survey known as the Myers-Briggs Type Indicator. This survey is designed to surface personal preferences on such basic topics as whether one prefers to get data from the world with one's senses or intuition, whether one evaluates that information from a thinking or a feeling approach, whether one is focused outward toward the world or inward toward the self, whether one is orderly or flexible in one's attitude toward life.[3] When Sue and Kevin understood the *other's* temperament, peace was restored.

The Myers-Briggs measures sixteen temperaments. It offers intriguing glimpses of the widely varying personal worldviews within the same culture. The following chart shows why it is important to be aware of the personal worldview filters through which we see things.

[3] Several books offer good introductions to understanding personality types, including: *Type Talk* by Otto Kroeger and Janet M. Thuesen, *Please Understand Me* by Keirsey and Bates, and *Gifts Differing* by Isabel Briggs-Myers.

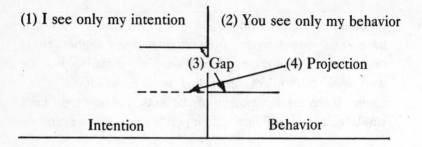

(1) I see only my intention | (2) You see only my behavior

(3) Gap   (4) Projection

Intention   Behavior

Behind every behavior is an intention. I intend to do something and then I do it. The problems we experience in communication are due to four factors. First, I see only my intention. I know what I intend to do/say/mean but I am not aware of how I am coming across to you. I don't see my behavior. Who among us can be looking in a mirror all the time? Second, you see only my behavior. You do not see my intention. You see what I am doing, but you don't know what intention lies behind my actions. Third, there is frequently a gap between what I intend and what I actually do. This is especially true when an emotional component is involved in the transaction. Have you ever decided to be reconciled with someone, only to have your attempts make matters worse? Fourth, we project our own intentions onto someone else's behavior. Without realizing it, we look at someone else's actions and ask, "What would *I* intend if I were doing that?" This is represented by the dotted line on the chart.

These four factors illustrate our personal worldview, how we perceive people and events from a set of given assumptions. The four factors are responsible for a vast amount of misunderstanding between persons. When I have projected my own intention onto your behavior and reacted to you, I am dealing with *my projection* instead of the *real you*. Let me illustrate this:

In the Myers-Briggs, one cluster of types is called SJ. These are sensory and judging people. Each of the sixteen types places different values on things. SJ's value people who are useful and responsible. Another cluster-type is called SP. These are sensory and perceptive people. What they value is spontaneity and freedom. Let's imagine a scene in which an SP man telephones an SJ woman and says, "Let's go to the movies. I'll pick you up in ten minutes."

"You will not!" she answers, thinking that is far too short notice.

"Why not? Are you already busy?" says the SP.

"No, I'm not busy. It's just that I need time to get ready for things."

"All right, make it thirty minutes, then."

"You're impossible!" she exclaims, hanging up.

What's going on here? The SP is intending to please the SJ, but unconsciously projects his own sense of time and spontaneity onto her. He can't see why it matters whether SJ has ten minutes' or ten days' notice. She should be glad he called. Or, "Maybe she doesn't like me and that's why she turned me down."

The SJ, on the other hand, projects her sense of responsibility onto the SP: He is irresponsible to ask for a date on such short notice. If he really cared for her he would have called before the last minute. Her conclusion: "He doesn't really like me. If he did, he would show more consideration."

The way to avoid communication glitches is this: *Clarify your intentions and provide feedback on the other's behavior.* If you alone see your intentions, then you are the one who must state your intentions when a glitch occurs. And if only you can see another's behavior, then you are the one who is going to have to provide him with feedback on how he is coming across to you. Whoever becomes aware that a glitch is going on is the one who has the responsibility to clarify his intentions or provide feedback on the other's behavior.

One day I came home swinging verbal fists. After a few minutes, my wife said, "Do you realize that you're trying to pick a fight? Is that what you intend?"

I thought about her question for a couple seconds and replied, "You know, I *have* been trying to pick a fight, but it's because I'm mad at someone else. I'm sorry. You're not the target. Give me a few minutes with the newspaper and I'll cool off." And an unnecessary fight was avoided.

Being vulnerable to personal worldviews requires that we keep a check on our projection by reminding ourselves that there are differences of temperament. Jesus had three injunctions that help in the business of defusing projection:

1. "Do not judge, or you too will be judged" (Matthew 7:1). Don't assume that your evaluation of another's behavior is accurate.
2. "If you forgive men when they sin against you, your heavenly Father will also forgive you" (Matthew 6:14). *Forgive* in Hebrew and Greek means literally "to send away." We send away another's sin when we forgive. If you send it away, it won't bother you anymore.
3. If it still bothers you that someone has sinned against you, "go and show him his fault, just between the two of you" (Matthew 18:15). Every time I have done this, I have found that the person I thought had sinned against me thought that I had sinned against him. We came to reconciliation quickly, clarifying intentions, providing feedback and offering and receiving forgiveness.

How It Works Culturally

Worldviews can get in our way culturally as well as personally. And when we are vulnerable to—open to—another person's cultural worldview we have a much better chance of communicating. Charles Kraft of Fuller Theological Seminary's School of World Mission worked up the chart on the following page to show that cultural assumptions lead to definite conclusions.

Notice the cultural feature of buying. Remember the American women and the Arab shopkeeper at the beginning of this chapter? Both women probably shared the American cultural assumption that making a purchase is an impersonal, economic transaction, concluding that it can be gotten over quickly without getting to know the seller. For whatever reasons, the first woman made a quick, impersonal purchase, paying the asking price. If she had noticed the shopkeeper's disdain toward her, she would probably have concluded that he was ungrateful, anti-American or chauvinistic. The second woman paid *less* than the asking price, but the shopkeeper seemed neither ungrateful, anti-American nor chauvinistic toward her. In fact, he seemed pleased. What made the difference?

Look at his assumptions about buying. As a member of the Third World, he probably held that buying is a social, person-to-person transaction. He would take time to establish relationships with his customer, expecting her to act similarly toward him. He would dicker over prices as much to further the relationship as to conclude the deal. To him, there was no deal if there was no relationship.

Think for a moment about the projection possibilities here. The shopkeeper could have projected onto the first woman

Cultural Feature	Assumption	Conclusion
Clothing	1. Immodest to go naked (U.S.A.)	1. Must wear clothes even to bed.
	2. One covers one's body only if hiding something (Gava people—Nigeria)	2. Go naked to prove yourself.
	3. For ornamentation only (Higi people—Nigeria)	3. Wear on "occasion" only. Rearrange or change in public.
Buying	1. Impersonal, economic transaction (U.S.A.)	1. Fixed prices. No interest in seller as person. Get it over with quickly.
	2. Social, person-to-person (Africa, Asia, Latin America)	2. Dicker over price. Establish personal relationship. Take time.
Youthfulness	1. Desirable (U.S.A.)	1. Look young, act young. Cosmetics.
	2. Tolerated, to be overcome (Africa)	2. Prove yourself mature. Don't act young.
Age	1. Undesirable (U.S.A.)	1. Dreaded. Old people unwanted.
	2. Desirable (Africa)	2. Old people revered.
Education	1. Primarily formal, outside home, teacher-centered (U.S.A.)	1. Formal schools. Hired specialists.
	2. Primarily informal, in the home, learner-centered, traditional (Africa)	2. Learn by doing. Discipleship. Proverbs and folk tales.
Family	1. Centered around spouses (U.S.A.)	1. Compatibility of spouses all-important.
	2. For the children (Africa)	2. Mother-child relationship paramount.
Rapid Change	1. Good, change = progress (U.S.A.)	1. Encourage rapid change and innovation.
	2. Threat to security (Africa)	2. Conservatism valued. Aim at stability.

that she wasn't interested in anyone whose skin color differed from hers, that she was rude, that she cared nothing for him as a person and that she disdained the proper way to do things. She, meanwhile, could have projected onto him that he was slow, unindustrious and, therefore, lazy, meddlesome or perhaps trying to put the make on her. In all likelihood, neither of these projections would have been accurate. But they would stand, with all the force of experiential reality, to determine each one's future assumptions about the category of person the other typified.

"Don't tell me that Arabs are gracious people," the first woman could have told the second, who would have disagreed. And they would have been talking about the *same* man.

Vulnerability to cultural worldview is the same as toward temperamental worldview. It requires that we suspend judgment, learn as much as we can about other peoples, forgive when we think we have been offended, check out with knowledgeable people what a confusing behavior might have meant and try to see things "through the other guy's eyes."

Is There a Biblical Worldview?

There is no question that the writers of the Bible shared the Hebrew worldview of the Old Testament as well as the Greek one in parts of the New Testament. Much of Bible interpretation[4] takes into account these cultural features. It helps, for example, to understand how the Jews accomplished courtship, engagement and matrimony. You will better understand the predicament of a young pregnant woman named Mary if

[4] Called "exegesis," a formal approach to the text in which background information, linguistic analysis, cultural details and who said what to whom makes it easier to get the sense of a given passage.

you learn these cultural matters. Is the Bible's cultural manner of marriage the way *we* should get married? No, the cultural features of the biblical people are not superior or inferior to ours. They are just different. There are historical, sociological, cultural and religious reasons why any society practices the worldview it has. None is particularly better than another.

A mistake to which modern biblical scholars can tend, however, is to relegate anything they do not understand to a *cultural* rather than a *real* explanation.[5]

We in the West have had strong opinions since the Enlightenment of the late 1700s about what is possible and impossible. If something cannot be scientifically verifiable, we tend to doubt its existence in the "real" world. We may be prepared to believe in the existence of God or heaven or hell or angels or demons, but those entities exist in another sphere, not down here on the surface of the planet.

When we *do* encounter data from the realm of the spiritual, we are prone to dismiss it with psychological or mythical or superstitious explanations. If you turned over in your sleep, opened your eyes and saw a hideous demon leering at you, would you have any boxes in your mind in which to park that piece of information? Would you be able to accept it as real?

I remember the first demon I ever ran into. Without quite realizing it, I also made myself vulnerable to a new (to me) biblical worldview.

Some Christian young adults brought a seventeen-year-old girl into my office, saying that she was affected by a demon. Well, I had never encountered a demon and tended to doubt their "real" existence. But I decided to humor these kids.

[5] A current book that deals with these issues with particular effectiveness is *Christianity with Power* by Charles H. Kraft.

Besides, they were deeply concerned for their friend and I wanted to honor that concern. So I decided to act as if the girl were demonized[6] and in biblical fashion began speaking to the demon they said was in her.

Nothing much happened for a while. After about ten minutes, however, there was a dramatic change: The girl began talking in a man's voice and with a theological vocabulary far beyond the sophistication of a teenager. The hair on the back of my neck came to attention. A major shift was taking place in my own worldview. Now *I*, too, believed that a demon was there.

For twenty minutes I told that demon to get out of her. It wasn't going, not on *my* say-so. I was about to concede that I was no match for this demon, when another dramatic thing happened: I simply became livid. Absolute anger seized me. I grasped the arms of my chair to keep from leaping over the coffee table. Through clenched teeth these words seethed out: *"That's it! I've had it with you! Get out!"* And it did. Instantly. The girl calmed down. The masculine voice left her. She spoke in her own words again. I was so shocked at my anger and at its effectiveness that I barely noticed the girl pinching herself, finding a new perception of herself, hardly daring to rejoice at the elimination of something that had plagued her since she was three years old.

That experience made a major change in my worldview. I began to read the biblical accounts of ministry to the demonized with new interest. "Good heavens! If there are any more of these things to bump into, I want to know what to do with

---

[6] The New Testament never uses the word *possessed*. Rather it usually uses the Greek word *diamonizomenous*, which is best translated "demonized," and which can indicate any degree of severity from minor harassment to severe control. Sometimes the text uses *en pneumati akatharto*, literally, "with an unclean spirit."

them." Demons, I discovered, are not dismissible as a cultural feature of a superstitious Bible-times society. That doesn't mean that there is a demon everywhere some people think there is. But it is a real option that must be considered.

A biblical worldview contains many factors that some Westerners find strange. A short list includes: Satan, demons, healing, miracles, the occult, supernatural gifts and angels. There are also significantly different views of natural factors such as time (cyclical and contemporaneous rather than sequential), space (created rather than chance-evolved), life (spiritual more significant than biological), decision-making (consensus rather than 51 percent democracy), values (faith more important than wealth), structures (new preferable to old), persons (some more important than others).

Vulnerability to a biblical worldview means taking these things seriously, granting them the possibility of reality and changing our concept of the real as we study and experience life.

Jesus' Worldview

Jesus' own worldview was sometimes at variance with that of His contemporaries. In other words, *His* biblical worldview differed from *their* biblical worldview. We have already discussed His concept of Scripture in the previous chapter. Here I want to focus on factors in His behavior and statements about Himself that even those who shared the same general worldview found startling.

It was not surprising to the Pharisees that someone could be affected by a demon. But it was shocking for them to hear this: "If I drive out demons by the Spirit of God, then the kingdom of God has come upon you" (Matthew 12:28). Jesus was making cosmic claims about Himself that were alarming to the Pharisees. Was He saying He was God? Who but God could cast out demons "by the Spirit of God"? He was backing up those claims with astonishing acts of power. To the Pharisees the term *Kingdom of God* held an overlay of political expectations. Further, they had been waiting for it for so long that when it appeared, they couldn't believe it.

The common people were surprised by Him, too. After He had taught the people, the account says, "the crowds were amazed at his teaching, because he taught as one who had authority, and not as their teachers of the law" (Matthew 7:28–29). The common people had heard lots of teaching before. But there was a quality about this teaching that amazed them.

Jesus' worldview showed up in His organization, too. He seemed to pay no attention to labels. He called a political traitor to be on His staff. This was surprising enough to an oppressed people. Then He called a couple of freedom fighters to join the team. Then Matthew and Simon and Judas . . . a perfect recipe for staff disunity. No one in his right mind would put together a working group with members so hostile to one another. What could He have been thinking of?

When He quoted from the Scriptures, He was always dragging up verses "inappropriate" to the situation facing them. Here was a flock of ne'er-do-wells sponging dinner off a just-conscripted-and-stunned Matthew. Jesus, criticized for tolerating their presence, responded, "It is not the healthy who need a doctor, but the sick. But go and learn what this means: 'I desire mercy, not sacrifice' " (Matthew 9:12, quoting Hosea 6:6).

At least four times Jesus gave demonstrative sermons to His followers about their pride. Luke says that at the Last Supper they were still arguing about who was the greatest. Jesus' response was to strip off His clothes and perform the ministrations of the lowest slave. You can bet this blew their world-view right out of their upper windows.

The people of Jesus' day knew all about dead persons. But they were stunned by Jesus' actions at funerals: He ruined every funeral He ever went to, even His own. I mean, it's hard to have a good funeral when the dead don't stay dead!

Worldviews went *tilt* whenever Jesus spoke or acted. He spoke out of a viewpoint that astonished people. He acted out of expectations that no one seemed to share. So familiar was He with His viewpoint and expectations that He was surprised when those around Him didn't share them: "Where is your faith?" He asked His disciples when they failed to rebuke the wind and the waves for themselves (Luke 8:25). And they were surprised that He was surprised.

I have a prayer taped to the back wall of my office closet. I see it when I hang up my coat in the mornings. "Lord, let me see as You see and love as You love." I pray this prayer because Jesus' worldview has impacted my mindset only peripherally. I don't see things as He does. Much of the time I don't *want* to see as He sees, much less love as He loves.

But it is a worldview I must embrace. When we see as He sees and love as He loves, we find our schedules get wounded, our wallets get wounded, our comfort gets wounded, our reputations get shredded and our pride gets obliterated. Vulnerability to Jesus' worldview involves one in losing one's life and therefore, of course, gaining it.

Jesus had and has a viewpoint on everything. Being vulnerable to that viewpoint requires action. The first step in discovering it is to want it. The second step is to ask for it. The third step is to put yourself in His shoes. Maybe we should start the next chapter with a procedure that has proven useful in accomplishing this third step.

5
Vulnerability to the Headship of Jesus

Being open to the risky step of submitting to Jesus is a process that requires time. We say glibly, "Jesus is Lord!" but when it comes to living this out most of us balk.

When I was eighteen and a freshman at the University of California, Santa Barbara, I accompanied an Episcopal college group to a conference in Colorado Springs. We chartered a bus and piled in for the sixteen-hour journey. Almost twenty years later the major benefit of that trip became evident and led into my being willing to be vulnerable to the headship of Jesus. It wasn't the conference that led to the breakthrough. It was a simple, five-step Scripture meditation process that one of the chaplains, Edward Crowther, shared with me to alleviate the boredom of the midnight ride across Utah. The steps are easily remembered by the five words that summarize them: *Pray, Read, Picture, Project, Resolve.*

Meditation in Five Steps

1. Pray. Pray that the Lord will open you to His Word and open His Word to you. Pray to see Jesus in His Word.

2. Read. Read a passage through two or three times so that the sequence of events is clear in your mind. This process works best with scenes from the historical books—Old Testament events, the Gospels, Acts—because events are digested more easily than concepts.

3. Picture.[1] Act like a TV camera and imagine what the scene must have looked like. See the events unfold as you would watch a film.

4. Project. In this step, you project yourself into the roles of the persons in the story. Be Peter as he faces the fact that he has caught no fish. Hear Jesus as He checks in with the Father and tells Peter to let down the net. Be Peter as he lets down the net doubtfully at Jesus' instructions. Imagine what it feels like to be him. Observe the result. Feel Peter fall to his knees and bid Jesus get away from him. See Jesus smile, lift Peter to his feet and promise He will make him a fisher of men. Think the thoughts Peter might have thought.

Projecting is the heart of the process. At this stage the Spirit speaks to your heart and mind. I never understood Pharisees until I had stood in their boots a number of times and felt their feelings and thought their thoughts about Jesus. I never understood key factors in the viewpoint of God until I had tried to see with Jesus' eyes. The almost unrelenting challenge Jesus presented to His disciples—simply by saying what He

[1] There is a misguided teaching running around the Christian community that it is spiritually unsound to utilize the imagination because cults encourage this kind of "seeing." Satan quoted Scripture at Jesus in the temptation. Does that mean we cannot quote Scripture because Satan did? Satan is a compulsive usurper, always creating false approximations of God's gifts. But this does not invalidate God's gifts. The Bible clearly states that the Father is a Spirit, yet it also states clearly that Jesus "saw" Him in action. What did Jesus see Him with, if not His imagination? Jesus Himself said He only did what He *saw* the Father doing. In Matthew 9:4, the Greek says, "But Jesus, *seeing* their thoughts, said. . . ." The imagination can be misused, certainly, but this is no reason to forbid its use. Let us be centered on the Lord in our use of it, and we will be safe.

said and doing what He did—was not real to me until I put myself face to face with Him in their heads.

5. *Resolve.* The first four steps almost invariably teach you something that requires a resolution: to change an attitude, a priority, a behavior, a belief, an opinion, a procedure or a relationship.

These five steps take about fifteen minutes to complete. If you want to gain the fullest benefit, take another fifteen minutes and write down what you have learned and resolved. I buy books of lined pages at the stationers called "Record" for this purpose. Over a dozen of them sit on my shelves as testimonials to the most valuable spiritual exercise I have discovered.

As I said, it was about twenty years after I learned these five steps that I began to use them. I started with the Gospel of John. Using this five-step meditation process about four days a week, it took me eighteen months to get through John. I was incredibly enriched by the encounters I had with the Lord as I entered deeply into His scenes.

But there was another learning that could not have been seen on any individual day of this exercise. One day the Holy Spirit put together something I had been encountering for months but could not precisely finger. Of all things, it came as a quasi-mathematical formula: F:S::S:B.

"As the Father is to the Son, so the Son is to the Believer." That was it. It gave immediate and full expression to a dynamic that had been prowling around the campfires of my mind for months as I had five-stepped through John. In sum: Jesus' relationship with the Father is the model for our relationship with Jesus. How Jesus heard, responded to, was intimate with, obeyed, served the glory of and was backed up by the Father is how we are to hear, respond to, be intimate with, obey, serve the glory of and be backed up by Jesus. Notice the similarities in these two columns of verses from John:

As the Father is to the Son	*So the Son is to the Believer*
"I tell you the truth, the Son can do nothing by himself; he can do only what he sees his Father doing." 5:19	"If a man remains in me and I in him, he will bear much fruit; apart from me you can do nothing."15:5
"I do nothing on my own but speak just what the Father has taught me." 8:28	"If anyone loves me, he will obey my teaching." 14:23
"As the Father has loved me . . ." 15:9	"So have I loved you." 15:9
"Just as I have obeyed my Father's commands and remain in his love . . ." 15:10	"If you obey my commands, you will remain in my love." 15:10
"Do not believe me unless I do what my Father does." 10:37	"I tell you the truth, anyone who has faith in me will do what I have been doing." 14:12
"And whoever accepts me accepts the one who sent me." 13:20	"Whoever accepts anyone I send accepts me." 13:20
"On that day you will realize that I am in my Father." 14:20	"You are in me, and I am in you." 14:20
"You in me." 17:23	"I in them." 17:23
"You gave me [the words]." 17:8	"For I gave them the words . . . and they accepted them." 17:8
"As the Father has sent me . . ." 20:21	"I am sending you." 20:21

This brief comparison is but the merest sample of a dynamic that saturates the Gospel of John. Jesus is not saying that we are to be like Him in *every* respect. Obviously there are many significant differences: He was preexistent; He was born of a virgin; He was sinless; He was the sacrifice for sin; He had the Spirit without measure; His union with the Father was untainted; He completely exemplified the Father. None of these is even remotely true of us.

But He is saying that we are to find the dynamics of our relationship with Him from His relationship with the Father; He is saying that our sent-ness by Him is prefigured in His sent-ness by the Father; He is saying that His love for us is modeled after the Father's love for Him; He is saying that His power will back us up as the Father's power backed Him up. Where He states our divergence from Him, He predicts that we will do *greater*—not lesser—things than He has done, because He is going back Home (John 14:12). And He thoroughly models the God-dependence and Spirit-fullness by which we can do the same things, and even greater things, than He.

Jesus radically challenges the average Christian's self-effacing, powerless self-image. He says, "Look, I have shown you how to depend on Me, how to let My power come through You, how to enjoy My love and Lordship. Now I want you to go to work." But we excuse ourselves and never get around to proving that the model He gave is effective.

Vulnerability to the headship of Jesus means looking Him in the eye and following what He tells you to do. It means saying, "Yes, I agree that You modeled effective relationship and ministry for me, and I'm going to follow that model." It means, "If You tell me to go heal my neighbor I will go." It means, "I will bask so extensively in Your love that others will be encouraged to believe that You love them that much, too." It means, "I accept being absolutely, radically dependent on

You for direction, empowerment and results." It means, "You really are in charge."

Years ago I pastored a small mission congregation in El Monte, California. At one point, someone gave us a no-strings-attached bequest of about $35,000. For several months the vestry discussed what to do with that money. I thought I heard the Lord say, *Give it away!* But no one else felt that was a good idea. One morning, preparing for another vestry meeting, I said, "Lord, what am I supposed to do about this bequest?" He said, *Write out your letter of resignation. Then propose once more that you give the money away. If it's voted down, submit your resignation.*

Later we will discuss the yardsticks available for screening true from false messages from God. But for now I can say that hearing this word from God took my breath away. After the shock toned down, I wrote out my letter of resignation. I was, however, in clear disagreement with the Lord about giving up my job over something so foolish as money. "Why not make it over something really important?" I asked. But God, not we ourselves, draws the lines of what is important. If He thinks it is significant enough for us to lose our lives/jobs/reputations over things we think unimportant, then His headship is at stake.

So I said at the meeting that night, "I don't think we need to hash this over again. I just feel that I should move once more that we give the bequest away. Is there a second?" Someone seconded it and we voted. For it! Unanimously. I couldn't believe it. I already had my fingers on the resignation in my briefcase. So we set up a formula and schedule by which to off-load our assets. And over the next few years, the greatest joy of our meetings was deciding whom to give our money to. Jesus knew that it was more blessed to give than to receive and wanted that blessedness for us.

In another example, I was reading in Romans one day when

the words caught my eye, "Owe no man any thing, but to love one another" (13:8, KJV). Well. Sue and I owed lots to the credit card people. What's more, I had felt that the Lord was urging us to tithe. To that point, we were giving only about three percent to the church. So I talked Sue into raising our pledge to seven percent as a step toward a full tithe and tearing up all our credit cards. We were a touch breathless.

Within weeks, our fifteen-year-old refrigerator began emitting ominous sounds. I knew we couldn't go get a new one on credit. So Sue took a one-pound coffee can, decorated it with a sign that said "Ice Box Bank," and we started putting "extra money" in it, which was a joke because we thought we had no extra money. A couple of months passed and the death rattles wooed a repairman to the house who confirmed that it was, indeed, death that awaited our machine, and not repair. We laid hands on the thing and prayed for longevity. Meanwhile I began to research new refrigerators, concluding, of course, that the most expensive model on the market was what we needed. About $780, I remember.

Finally, our old machine strangled itself one day in our absence. We opened the Ice Box Bank and were surprised at how the occasional dollar had added up. With that, plus what we had in the checkbook, we went and paid *cash* for the new fridge. Cash! C-a-s-h. We had never paid cash for anything more expensive than a pair of shoes. At the end of the year I was delighted to up my pledge to a full ten percent, widely and enthusiastically telling people, "You can't pay me *not* to tithe."

That's the headship of Jesus. He loves us. He knows how to run our lives. He invites us to obey Him, trusting, and He always blesses the obedience. That's how He ran *His* life, proving to us that it works. When we collaborate with Him, we also prove that it works.

Sometimes His demands can be heart-stopping. I found myself complaining to Him one day that my leadership of our prayer and praise group was ineffective. The problem was that the numbers of those attending declined steadily. It was embarrassing: I was supposed to be a leader in charismatic renewal and I couldn't even sustain my own group's interest.

Came the reply, *I want Sunday mornings.*

Oh, no! I thought. *He'll ruin them.* I wished I could pretend that I didn't know what He meant, but I did know. He wanted to control what went on in the worship services.

Over the next few years a pattern of guidance began to emerge that I have heard called "the military method" of guidance. On a parade ground, the marchers are given a command of *preparation* followed by a command of *execution:* "Raheeeeeet . . . Face!" An idle thought would waft through my mind on occasion. It had the force of "wouldn't it be interesting if someday. . . ." That was the command of preparation. About a month later, smack in the middle of a worship service, would come the command of execution. With a gasp I would realize the preparatory nature of that funny little thought a month before. Sometimes there was a much shorter time lapse between preparation and execution.

One Sunday, for instance, I was standing at the altar praying for God to consecrate the Communion elements when I became aware that a line had been knocking at my mind for several minutes: "And a little child shall lead them." As I finished the prayer, I paused long enough to ask, *What's this all about—"A little child shall lead them"?* Immediately He said, *Give the plate to a child to administer the bread.*

Oh, great! I could already read the letter of complaint someone would send to my bishop: "And you know what he did during Communion the other day?"

But if I pondered it, I knew I would chicken out. So I

wheeled around and called the first child my eyes landed on. She came timidly to the altar and I explained that she was to give the bread to the people, showing her how to do it and telling her what to say. Then I stood back to watch. And it was charming, watching this innocent child communicate the bread to the people. But I didn't think it was worth the risk of a complaint until the grandfather of the child came forward. As she placed the bread in his hand, I saw what the command had been all about. This man had been able to sidestep me and my sermons for years, but he couldn't sidestep his granddaughter. He began to weep. He met God right there at the altar rail. The Head of the Church had tucked his 99 sheep safely in the fold and had gone after His one lost sheep.

Every one of the scores of times I have told this story tears come to my eyes. I tell you, it would be worth a thousand complaints of unconventionality for results like that.

Our Sunday services are quite unlike anything you will find in the "normal" Episcopal church. But I don't care very much anymore. Every Sunday people get healed, they become intimate with God and with each other, they minister and are ministered to. And two or three times a year, Jesus initiates something *else,* as though He is never satisfied with the status quo.

Vulnerability to Jesus' headship may on occasion mean suffering. His vulnerability to the Father in Gethsemane meant the most inhumane suffering man had devised. The mere contemplation of that suffering was itself so grievous that He sweated blood.

But His final redemptive act of suffering was not the first discomfort He had endured. Once in Nazareth I was looking into "the Grotto of the Holy Family" when the Spirit brought to mind the text from Hebrews 2:10, "He was made perfect through suffering." I replied, *This is the wrong city for You to*

give me that verse in, Lord. He didn't suffer here. In the next few
seconds I had flashes of insight that pictured Jesus at, say, 21,
finishing His carpentry one day, walking out of town into the
surrounding fields, looking up to heaven and saying, "Now,
Father?"

Not yet, Son.

Again at 25 and 28 He did the same. Finally, at thirty, He
said, "Father, I trust in Your perfect will. It makes no difference to Me when I begin My ministry."

To which the Father could answer, *Now, Son!*

All of Jesus' boyhood contemporaries in Nazareth had been
at their life's work for fifteen years before He began His. Part
of the perfection He accomplished came through the suffering
of waiting. Jesus' usefulness to the Father was, in part,
founded on His not having an agenda of His own. That was
what He had to give up. And if it took Him some years to do
so, it's liable to take us awhile, too.

When our ambition and His headship clash, we can take a
new step into growth. Even ambition for Jesus and His causes
must give way to obedience to Jesus and His headship. It is
still true that " 'my thoughts are not your thoughts, neither
are your ways my ways,' declares the Lord" (Isaiah 55:8).
What makes perfect sense to us as a means of achieving His
glory often clashes with His perspective.

David and King Saul demonstrate this. Over and over we
see that David "inquired of the Lord," whereas Saul would
do what seemed best to him. On the few occasions when Saul
inquired of the Lord, his obedience was partial. It was for this
that he was rejected as king. But David sought the Lord,
inquiring of Him, hearing Him and for the most part obeying
Him. Maybe one reason the Father decided that Jesus would
be of the lineage of David relates to this, for we have seen

Jesus' own statement that He did only what He saw the Father doing.

I have, for the last six years, taken the last Tuesday of the month as a prayer day, an uninterrupted time of trying to listen to the Lord. Being a bit hyperactive and loving the outdoors, I try to go to some mountain, usually within an hour's drive. I look for flat-topped mountains upon which I can walk to and fro, enjoy the scenery and settle down to listening.

Once, on the way to one such mountain, the negative self-talk[2] was intense: "Why are you wasting time up here when you could be doing something useful at your office? You're just up here because you like the mountains. Think of all the administrative needs you are abandoning by being up here." This line of thought finally immobilized me. I really wanted to do the Lord's will, but I was confused at that point what His will was. I almost decided to go back to the office when it occurred to me to ask God.

"What do You think, Lord?"

Almost immediately the impression "Jeremiah 10" came into my thoughts. I stopped, opened my Bible to Jeremiah chapter 10 and started reading. At verse 21, I got the answer: "The shepherds are senseless and do not inquire of the Lord; so they do not prosper and all their flock is scattered." I am a shepherd. I want my congregation to prosper. I want it to be in unity. My whole purpose for being on the mountain was to inquire of the Lord. So it was with great confidence that I continued to the place where I was going to pray. That day the Lord gave me the church plan for the entire year.

What kinds of suffering might vulnerability to Jesus' headship entail? As with Him, waiting is one. I remember reading that Senate chaplain Richard Halverson tearfully told the Lord he didn't mind spending his entire ministry in some village as

[2] To be discussed in chapter 7 on spiritual warfare.

long as he was sure the Lord wanted him there. He was ambitious, gifted and capable. But he wanted to stay under the headship of Jesus rather than promote himself. If it is God's work we strive to accomplish, doesn't it make sense that He can get us to the right place in the right time by the right means to fulfill His own plan? How can we expect to be given charge of the greater things if we haven't satisfied Him in the lesser ones?

Another kind of suffering concerns misunderstanding. The gap between finitude and infinitude involves us regularly in lack of understanding. That should be expected. My experience is that God does not often take me into His counsel. Rather, He issues orders and keeps His own counsel. Does that mean that I give up the pursuit of understanding? No, Paul himself wrote fourteen times "that ye may understand." But God seems to draw a line between understanding *more* and understanding *everything*. I have often been given commands without so much as a wisp of rationale. If I demand to see the rationale before complying with the command, He shuts up. But if I go ahead with obedience, later I invariably see at least something of the rationale for the order, having seen what my obedience accomplished. We need to check out our marching orders against Scripture, but we do not need to understand them.

At times the suffering of misunderstanding comes when you have heard something from the Lord, you have checked it out against Scripture, you have peace and you act. Before you see results you are attacked for what you did. What can you say? You don't *know* why you did it, except that you thought the Lord told you to. If that doesn't satisfy the complainant, silence is the next step. That hurts. I think it also hurt the One who "opened not His mouth."

It is easy to rationalize that our reputations are more important than our obedience. But that is not how Jesus approached the issue. Look, for example, at His behavior in John 6. Over and over in that chapter He told the people that they must eat His flesh and drink His blood if they were to have eternal life. This was offensive to Jews. *No* blood was to be consumed, especially not the blood of a human (see Leviticus 7:26, 17:10–14).

> On hearing it, many of his disciples said, "This is a hard teaching. Who can accept it?" Aware that his disciples were grumbling about this, Jesus said to them, "Does this offend you? What if you see the Son of Man ascend to where he was before! The Spirit gives life; the flesh counts for nothing. The words I have spoken to you are spirit and they are life. Yet there are some of you who do not believe."   John 6:60–64

Jesus had permission from the Father to give them a clue but not to resolve their offense. To resolve their offense would be to clarify something like this: "Do not be dismayed by this. What I really mean is that you will take bread and wine and consume them for My body and blood. I was going to tell you later, but seeing your distress, I've decided to tell you now." No, the closest He came was to give them a clue: "The Spirit gives life; the flesh counts for nothing." Their flesh, their human understanding, was giving them great distress at what He was saying. But if they were to check with their spirits, they would find some sort of assurance that, in spite of their distaste for His words, things would somehow come right. In my experience, that assurance is perceived as peace.[3]

God is willing to give assurance, but not necessarily the kind we want. The disciples failed to check with His kind of assurance: "From this time many of his disciples turned back

---

[3] What I mean by peace will be explained more fully in chapter 8 on guidance.

and no longer followed him" (verse 66). These were disciples, followers, believers who were leaving Him. They had resisted others' calling Him crazy and demonized and megalomaniacal, but now He had gone too far. Still Jesus refused to clarify. Instead, Jesus said to the Twelve, "You do not want to leave too, do you?" (verse 67).

Notice the stakes. Far more than His reputation was at issue now. The Twelve were Jesus' Isaac. Just as Abraham had to be the father of nations through Isaac and no one else but Isaac (Genesis 21:12), so Jesus had to build His Church through the Twelve. As Abraham had been challenged by God to sacrifice Isaac, so Jesus was challenged to be willing to release the Twelve. It was as though He was saying, "This issue is nonnegotiable. You either believe Me without seeing how the matter is resolved or you disbelieve Me and go your way."

At another level, it was as though the Father was saying to Jesus, "This issue is nonnegotiable. Either You command and receive their trust or You let them go." Jesus was passing the test. What about the disciples? "Simon Peter answered him, 'Lord, to whom shall we go? You have the words of eternal life. We believe and know that you are the Holy One of God!" (verses 68–69). I think I hear overtones that they would have *liked* to go somewhere, but where? To go anywhere else would be to leave Him, whom they had come to believe was the Holy One of God. It was as though they were thinking, "We don't like what You're saying one bit; we don't understand it; it repels us; but the option is unacceptable. For better or worse, we cannot leave You."

Jesus' reputation. The Twelve's reputations. The disciples' reputations who left. God's reputation. All were at stake in this confrontation.

I would like to close this chapter leaving you to mull over these questions: What are the nonnegotiables in your life? Where did you get them?

6
Vulnerability to Self

Having created us in His image, God is determined to reveal His image in us, do His works through us and speak His words through us. He is not exclusively incarnationalist, for He reserves to Himself the managing of the galaxies, the seasons, even the number of hairs on our heads without our help. But He places a very significant amount of human interaction in human hands, and He seems always eager to increase rather than decrease this mode of operation.

Having made the decision to incarnate Himself in us, God makes Himself vulnerable to our limitations: limitations of temperament, personal history, giftedness, maturity, understanding and agreeability, for example. My assumption is that He has reconciled Himself to this manner of working and that we should, too.

We were about halfway through the Sunday service when he said it. It was a glorious day. The music was magnificent, I had preached what I thought was a good sermon, the people were responsive and the bishop had just concluded the ceremony instituting me as the new rector of St. Jude's. Then he said it: "Your new rector is an everyday, garden-variety sort of priest."

75

I snapped a look at him. How dare he call me "everyday, garden-variety"! I smiled quickly, however, swallowing the anger and hoping that no one noticed the flush on my face. But I was doing a slow burn for the rest of the day, for I could not ignore the remark. I was so busy getting settled into my new position that I didn't deal with the bishop's comment for a couple of weeks.

Finally I got around to it, grousing to the Lord, "Lord, I forgive the bishop for calling me those things, but I'd be lying if I told You I *feel* forgiving toward him. You know that at this point forgiveness is solely an act of the will." I knew that I would eventually feel forgiving, for I have found it to be true that "feelings follow faith." I was congratulating myself for doing the right thing in offering willful, obedient forgiveness when I got another surprise: *But I told him to say that. I want to show what I can do through everyday, garden-variety sorts of people.*

Somehow it was hard to take this as good news. I just sat there. A maelstrom of conflicting thoughts about myself swirled through me.

"Almighty God thinks I'm nothing special," I said.

"Well, I'm not!" I answered.

"What kinds of things can He do through the likes of me?"

"Nothing special."

"Who says?"

"*He* says!"

"No, He didn't. He said Mike Flynn was nothing special but He can do great things through the people who are far from special."

I didn't know whether to be hurt or happy. I'd like to say that I got the thing resolved quickly. But for a couple of years I smarted over the bishop's comment, virtually forgetting what God had said about it. Every once in a while I would slander the bishop in some way, which resulted in having to ask for his forgiveness.

Meanwhile, I wasn't exactly the picture of specialness. I was ordinary and my work was ordinary. It was as though the bishop's comment had predicted the quality of my pastorate. But then the Lord brought to mind the manner in which I had quit smoking, for in that experience was a clue for my present circumstance.

I had started smoking in college and had puffed my way through seminary and several years of ministry. I had tried to quit numerous times and read books proving what I already knew: Cigarettes were bad for me. But that didn't motivate me to stay off cigarettes. I had rationed them, scheduled them and made bets about quitting them. And I had puffed right along.

One day, while I was absentmindedly thinking about my smoking, there came this thought:

Why don't you die to yourself as a smoker?

"That's what I've been trying to do!"

No, you've been trying to quit smoking, came the reply.

"I thought they were the same," I answered. "How do you die to yourself as a smoker?"

Accept yourself as a smoker.

"I'd *never* quit if I did that. What's Your plan 'B'?"

But, of course, silence was the reply. Well, I had tried everything else. I decided I might as well try this. So the next morning I hid myself in our bathroom, looked into the mirror and said, "Flynn, you smoker, I accept you." I almost felt like spitting in disgust, but I kept it up. "I accept you. I accept you in spite of this habit. I accept that you're addicted, controlled by cigarettes. I accept that you burn holes in your clothing. I accept that you're damaging your body by their use. I accept that your mouth is a hundred and forty degrees after you smoke and that your night vision is cut by forty percent. I accept that you spend significant money on cigarettes that could be spent elsewhere. I accept that you can't do anything very long unless you have a cigarette."

That night, I repeated and elaborated upon the statements of acceptance I made to myself. And I set my will to follow this to some conclusion. This brought me face to face with myself each morning and night.

On about the fourth day, I realized that I really had to *mean* what I was saying. That is, acceptance meant that I would no longer withhold commendation or affection from myself because I smoked. It meant that I would have to cease berating myself because of the smoking. It meant that I had to *accept* myself in spite of the fact that I smoked. Slowly I began to realize what it was going to mean to die to my condemnation of myself as a smoker. Paul said, "I die daily." I could begin to see a daily death awaiting me as I foresaw continued smoking for which I would refuse to condemn or reject or censure myself.

The *I* was the operative word here. My condemnation of myself was sinfully self-centered. So the very first task was to *die to myself,* to my egoistic self-condemnation.

All the while, something in me was complaining, "This is all wrong! This is not the way to deal with something negative." And I more than half believed it. But I was committed to doing this acceptance thing through to a conclusion of some kind, so I continued.

A couple of days into the second week I had a conversation with the director of a nearby smoking clinic. He told me that people stop smoking the same way they start: by changing their self-image.

"You had to overcome terrific natural distaste for tobacco in order to become habituated," he said. "What got you over that distaste was what cigarettes were going to do for your image of yourself. They would make you more urbane, tough, sophisticated, collected or whatever. The trick is to construct a new self-image that *in*cludes being all the things you want to be while *ex*cluding cigarettes."

That made sense. Thereafter, in addition to making acceptance statements to myself morning and night, I sat down and imagined myself in all the situations in which I normally smoked. I saw myself as relaxed, comfortable and engaging, but I saw myself not smoking. I did that for the second week.

Then a remarkable thing occurred: At the end of that week, I felt as though I could quit.

One of the books I had read suggested that the night before you quit smoking you chain-smoke as many as you can, plus one. In my case, it was twelve. After gagging halfway through the twelfth cigarette, I snuffed it out and emptied the ashtray. The feeling in my mouth carried me through the first few days of nicotine withdrawal. My career with smoking was over.

The above is a dangerous concept unless it has a solid theological underpinning. We hate ourselves for our weaknesses, but God doesn't. He has made Himself vulnerable to our weaknesses and accepts us with our flaws. When we begin to do that, too, when we insist that our false images of strength *die* a bit every day, then, with one of God's ironic turns, we actually have a better chance of change.

Without this underpinning the concept of accepting our weaknesses is open to abuse. Most useful things are abusable. But I wish to clarify the parameters for the use of this concept, for it is severely limited in its usability.

The following drawing is scandalously simple. It ignores all manner of better ways to conceive of the dynamics of human personality. But I think it correctly indicates a real phenomenon. If something unwelcome is found in the peripheral self,

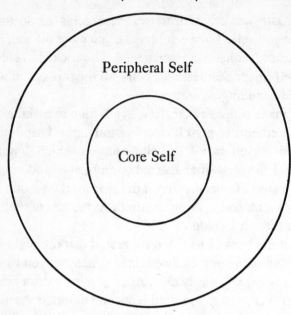

Peripheral Self

Core Self

it can be dealt with by repentance, study, discipline and prayer. "O God, I'm sorry. I've seen that this is wrong. I'm going to make every effort to triumph over this. Please help me." This approach will work for a great number of problems for relatively healthy people.[1]

If you have done and redone repentance, study, discipline and prayer, however, and there is still no good result, one option to consider is to die to the thing that has been haunting you by accepting yourself with it. My experience of myself is that matters of the core self do not respond to the methods by which I deal with peripheral matters. If I ask, "O God, take

---

[1] I must underline here that these methods of dealing with peripheral and core issues are not substitutes for counseling—professional and lay—or inner healing or deliverance or medication. I do not mean to oversimplify issues for persons who have been abused, for example, and require extensive therapy.

away my sin," a sin coming out of peripheral weakness, He is liable to do it. But if I ask, "O God, take away my self," He won't. For whatever reasons, my smoking was part of my core self.

This cannot be seen as a gimmick by which to get free of chains. You have to mean it when you tell yourself that you are accepting yourself with it. It really is a dying. Several of the things I have dealt with this way have been eliminated from my behavior, but some of the things I have accepted are still very much with me.

Well. Having been reminded of all that, I turned my attention to being an "everyday, garden-variety sort of priest." In fairly short order, I accepted it as the truth. Then a surprise came.

Having embraced ordinariness, it ceased to be an issue. My ordinariness did not go away, it just ceased to be important. What did increase in importance was the Lord's statement *I want to show what I can do through everyday, garden-variety sorts of people.* It was at that point that the Lord led me to discover, field-test, incorporate and export a theology and practice of ministry we had encountered from John Wimber.

In very short order, we at St. Jude's have begun to see the Lord do things through us we hadn't seen before. There are healings—physical, emotional, relational. There is an authority in team teaching that wins us favor in the hearts of our hearers when we go on the road.

So we are back to the question of vulnerability because that is at the heart of the change we saw.

What is vulnerability to self? First, it is the acceptance of God's plan to reveal Himself through people. God has chosen to use the likes of you. But with a condition: He will not use you if you try to run things on your own.

Second, we must embrace incarnation in all its specificity.

This involves an enormous *catalog of types of people* including worldviews, personal histories, temperaments, natural abilities, spiritual giftedness, sexes, educational levels and relational styles.

Third, we must carry incarnational specificity to the particulars. What has God created in each of us? "We accept others in direct proportion to how much we accept ourselves," the saying goes. The flip side of that is, "We reject others in direct proportion to how much we reject ourselves."

Notice the people you get angry at. Nine times out of ten you get angry at someone who touches off something in you that you haven't yet dealt with. Some years ago, the back of my mind was telling me that I was drinking too much wine, but I ignored it. So the Lord sent two persons into my office who had trouble with alcohol. The first one I didn't help at all. He smelled of a three-day binge. Oh, I said all the right things, but beneath the level of my words was flowing another dynamic—anger—and he picked up on it, going away unhelped because he was unaccepted.

The second man had conquered alcohol seven years before, but had a current difficulty he needed counsel on. I found myself angry at him, then suddenly realized that I feared him because he had faced and dealt with something I hadn't even had the courage to look at. I asked him if he minded coming back a week later. He agreed. By the time he got into his car I was on my knees asking, "Lord, am I an alcoholic?" It turns out that I wasn't an alcoholic in the sense of being allergic to alcohol, but I was consuming too much of the stuff. Once the problem was handled in me, I could relate acceptingly and helpfully with the second man and other alcoholics.

It also helps to notice who gets angry at you. Once you realize there is something about you that threatens someone, you can abandon defensiveness, be filled with compassion and seek ways to relieve them of the self-rejection.

Fourth, you can try to see yourself through God's eyes. Once in a quiet time the Lord showed me a picture of myself covered by a single layer of gauze.

"Lord, I could never hide under that gauze, could I! It's so diaphanous that I can see right through it. I can clearly see myself under it."

The gauze is Jesus, the Lord said.

The Lord was saying He could see nothing of me except through Jesus. When He looks at me, He sees Jesus first, and He sees me *in* Jesus. Nothing about me is visible to God without the covering of Jesus. It is a mindset He keeps. He has "made us accepted in the beloved" (Ephesians 1:6, KJV). Is Jesus acceptable? Then so am I.

Sometimes we have to take steps to appropriate this acceptance. I decided to meditate on Ephesians 1:6, but was stalled because it is a concept instead of an event. The five steps of meditation work best for me if I can put myself into an event.

"Help me, Lord," I prayed. Then it occurred to me to put myself in the Father's shoes on the day of the Ascension to see how He regarded Jesus, in whom I have been made acceptable. It felt presumptuous to be sitting on the throne of glory, but I believed it was O.K. to put that aside for the sake of the experiment. I'll frame the experience in the present tense. It's difficult, but here goes.

I am seeing things as God almighty. Here I am, sitting on My throne. This is a great day, for in a few minutes, My Son, who has been separated from Me for more than thirty years—Oh, how I have missed His immediate presence!—is going to return. At the moment He is finishing His comments to the disciples on the hillside opposite the Temple. My Spirit will now lift Him into the clouds. Ah, there He is now. The avenue is banked with high bleachers, filled with saints and angels, to whom I give a nod as Jesus begins the trek down the street toward the throne.

Wild, tumultuous, joyous mountains of praise bombard Jesus as He walks down the boulevard. The saints are shouting, "He is worthy!" and the angels are singing, "Glory to God." While all the host of heaven is worshiping Him, I monitor Myself for My own reactions to Him. I notice two things. First, I notice My *opinion* of Him. He did everything I sent Him to do. He lived for Me and for others. He was unselfish. He was obedient, even unto death. He never failed in faith or love. Yes, He is altogether worthy of all laud.

The second thing I notice is My *feelings* for Him. Oh, how I love Him! Oh, how proud I am of Him. It nearly killed Me to make Him the sacrifice for sin, and how nobly, how obediently, how courageously He bore it. He is My own heart come home. Now He's getting closer. I can hardly wait until He gets here, for I am going to throw My arms around Him for a thousand years before I do anything else.

Now Jesus ascends the steps to the dais on which the throne rests. As He reaches the top step, He pauses for a second before covering the remaining few feet to the throne where I am seated. . . .

Here the viewpoint suddenly shifts. Now, we are in Jesus, approaching the Father on His throne. (*I'm trying not to fight this, just receive it.*)

There He waits for Me, filled with these wonderful opinions of Me and yearning to satisfy His feelings for Me. (*This isn't right! These things belong to Jesus alone. It's a travesty for me to appropriate them for myself.*) I can see the unconditional approval and affection in His eyes. The acclaim of the hosts is ringing in My ears and through My soul. (*I don't deserve this!*

*But I hear the Father say in my mind that He wants me to realize
how He sees Jesus.)*

Just as I reach the foot of the throne, He stands and swoops
Me up onto His chest. Once again I feel Him surging through
Me, as it was before I went to earth. But there is a difference
now. The joy is fuller, if that is possible; the fact that I am a
body now makes an eternal difference in how I perceive and
feel Him. "O Father, it is done indeed. I am home again. It
was worth it. Thank You for sustaining me, for keeping Me,
for filling Me, for using Me, for guiding Me, for loving and
loving and loving Me. . . ."

And that was the way of it. I had learned a lot. For all of us.

It is the Father's pleasure to ascribe to you the deserved
worth of Jesus. Is Jesus worthy? Then so are you. Is Jesus
accepted? Then so are you. Is Jesus beautiful? Then so are
you. Paul had a particularly good grasp of this concept, using
the phrase *in Christ* more than eighty times. In Him, you *are*
perfect.

The fifth thing we can do is to accept God's acceptance of
us. This starts as an act of the will. There are two big lies in
our society today. The first is, "If it isn't logical, it isn't so."
The second is, "If I don't feel it, it isn't so." Both lies appeal
to our sense of integrity and honesty. "I'd *like* to believe," we
say, "but I don't understand it, so I can't be sure if it's true,"
or, "I just don't feel it, so it can't be true. I certainly don't
want to fake something so important as belief."

Those two lies keep millions from a living relationship with
God; they keep those already in relationship with Him from
the abundance of the life He promised. Faith is not a matter
of intellect. Nor is it a matter of emotion. It is centered in the
will, which can operate perfectly satisfactorily whether you
understand something or not and whether it feels good to you
or it doesn't.

The function of the will is to make decisions.

"Lord, I decide to accept Your acceptance of me. I decide to accept myself, because You do. I decide to take myself off probation. I decide to affirm myself in every particular, including my physical appearance and my history and my abilities. I decide to accept that Jesus fully paid off every sin I have committed or will commit so I don't have to pay them off myself. I decide that You like me and I decide to like myself. I decide that I am perfect in Your eyes because Jesus is perfect. I decide that improvement rests on a foundation of acceptance rather than stretching toward a goal of acceptance. I decide that this is all wonderfully, gloriously true."

Think how much easier it is for God to get His work done through someone who believes these things. If He's not always battling your self-rejection tooth and nail, He can get on with the positive things He has chosen to accomplish through you. When you get past wringing your hands over what a rotten witness you are, you can relax and let the Lord bump you into those He has appointed you to befriend.

I was trying to express this to a group once when a woman protested, "I don't want to be somebody *in Christ;* I want to be somebody *by myself.*" I smiled at her and paused before I answered, waiting for the Lord to give me His viewpoint. What came to mind was a favorite quip: "God doesn't love you because you are lovable but because He's a lover." Expanding on that I said, "If God loved you because you deserved it, His love would be a shaky thing because it would cease the moment you ceased to deserve it. The foundation of your being loved does not reside in you but in Him, and He never changes. He loves you because He is a lover. What's more, He insists that His love be a gift. If He loved you because you deserved it, His love would be a payment of some kind and that would commercialize it. Rather, He insists that it be a gift—unearnable and unpaybackable. You can receive or reject it. And I acknowledge that it is humbling to receive it."

The woman's problem was pride. What I said in an earlier chapter is worth repeating and expanding on: If you want to "be somebody" on your own, then I haven't much encouragement for you. As Norman Grubb says, "The goal in life is not to *be somebody* but to *contain Someone.*" Isn't that what it means to be a "jar of clay" (2 Corinthians 4:7)? I have found that the containing and giving forth of Jesus Christ is the most affirming, fulfilling and satisfying dynamic of my life. Somehow as I try to give *Him* forth, He mobilizes the best of *me*. I think that's an example of gaining one's life by losing it.

If I insist on being somebody on my own, I find that I become less, not more. My *self* shrinks as I push myself upon God or the world demanding affirmation. The more I grab for affirmation the more it slips through my fingers. But if I am willing to accept the status of being valued because of my identification with Jesus Christ and if I seek to display Him in my attitudes and actions and if I believe that He knows how to reveal Himself through my uniqueness, then I can relax and let blessing come to me on its own rather than force it through my door in a chokehold.

I may not be "special" but I am unique. Jesus looks different on me than on you: I "wear" Him one way and you "wear" Him another. Thank God! One of any of us is enough. Part of the "unsearchable riches of Christ" is that He can manifest Himself through every person on earth and never duplicate His revelation. *That's why it is so important that your particular combination of natural and spiritual gifts be made available to the world.* Christ can be and do through you in ways He cannot be or do through anyone else on earth.

A friend of mine who plays with computer math figured that

if each of the 23 spiritual gifts had ten levels, there would be $25,852,016,738,884,976,640,000^2$ possible combinations. That's five trillion times the world's current population. With all those combinations to choose from, isn't it reasonable that God's particular apportionment to you has been well-considered? Would He choose a combination that wasn't needed in your particular environment?

We slander the wisdom of God when we say, "If only. . . ."

"If only I were blond."

"If only I were brighter."

"If only I had more education."

"If only I were married."

"If only I could teach/lead/preach/heal/sing/cook/speak like Fred/Jane/Bill/Sue/John/Mary Ann/Roger."

If God were interested in cloning, I suppose He would have cloned us. But He is interested in incarnational revelation, and there is vastly too much of Him to be revealed to waste opportunities through duplication. One of the most useful tasks that can benefit the Kingdom of God is for you to ask— and answer at a length of not fewer than a dozen pages— "Who am I?" The more you know who you are, the clearer will be the vision of what God desires to do through you. He has incarnated Himself in you for a purpose. What is it?

If you begin to find out who you are, you will discover that someone else has begun to discover who you are, too; that other one is your enemy, the devil. He has created an array of dynamics by which to keep you off-balance lest you put him off-balance. In the next chapter we will look at these in considerable detail.

---

[2] For those of you who want to be able to say it: 25 sextillion, 852 quintillion, 16 quadrillion, 738 trillion, 884 billion, 976 million, 640 thousand.

7
Vulnerability to Spiritual Warfare

"Come, Holy Spirit. Now let's just wait on the Lord and see if He will tell us what's on His heart to do this evening." Silence: 45 seconds.

"O.K., I think the Lord wants to heal a woman with arthritis in her right hip. Is there someone here who fits that description?" No response: 20 seconds. (*You missed it, Mike. That wasn't from the Lord. You produced that out of your own mind.*)

"O.K., let's wait on that one a bit." Pause: 10 seconds. "There's also a woman here with a small lump on the right side of her right breast. Would that person please raise her hand?" No response: 30 seconds. (*Now you're in trouble. These people are going to know that you are a phony.*)

"I also have the impression that there is a man here in his fifties who has bursitis in his right shoulder." No response: 15 seconds. (*You sinner! This isn't working because you're a rotten sinner.*) "I think that you've had this condition for about one year." No response: 10 seconds. (*Why don't you just shut down this enterprise in fakery and get out of here?*)

I was slowly walking back and forth before the group, trying desperately to relax so I could hear from the Lord. But the accusations in my mind were coming furiously. I knew they were accusations. I knew they were the attempts of the enemy to sabotage what God was trying to do that night. But they were so believable!

My eyes found some of the members of my seven-person team. But they just looked at me. *I* was supposed to be the expert. They had no help for me. I looked to the Lord again, and it seemed in the flicky way the imagination works that He put His hand over His lower stomach and the word *colitis* came to mind. (*Don't do it! It's not working tonight! You're just going to make it worse.*) I said, "There is a woman here in her mid-thirties who has had a problem with colitis for the last five years. I believe God wants to heal you of that condition. Would you please come forward?" No response. The 75 people present were beginning to shift uncomfortably. I had been teaching them for an hour in this first of two sessions. It was Friday night. Our practice is never to teach without ministering, and I was trying to get the ministry time going.

Trying desperately to look confident, I walked back and forth a couple more times. I mentioned another condition. Again, no response. (*Give it up! You always knew this would happen, and now it has. You're finished.*) I had never had such a miserable response. The idea of shingles wafted across my mind with all the force of a tiny feather. I sighed internally. "Is there someone here who is suffering from shingles? You've got a band of affected area across your entire chest and half-way 'round the left side of your back." Suddenly a man who looked to be in his sixties stood up and came down the aisle. I could have kissed him. I put one of my team members with him, and he was relieved of pain within moments.

There followed a ministry time in which more than thirty people were prayed for. During that time, each one of the persons with the conditions I had seen in the Spirit came up front, confessing they were the ones, but had been embarrassed to come forward when their condition had been mentioned.

The next week, the pastor of the church where we had been ministering wrote, saying,

> Praise the Lord for last Friday and Saturday! At the Sunday evening service we had a testimony time which I thought would never end—because so many people were thanking the Lord for their healings the day or two before! The words of knowledge were right on, and the healings were taking place accordingly, and some even beyond the word of knowledge. Indeed Jesus was walking up and down the aisles and across the rows of pews doing His great work!
>
> Some of the reported healings that come to my mind are shingles, a bad knee that caused a painful limp, a rash on the hand, a left eye, arthritis, a serious back and neck injury, and many others.

I mention the event as a prime example of spiritual warfare.[1]

Not too long after being filled with the Spirit in 1972, I ran across a quote from (I believe it was) Andrew Murray that went, "One does not take the Holy Spirit seriously without eventually having to take the unholy spirit seriously also."

"Nonsense!" I protested. I didn't see any reason for having to focus on evil. Gradually, however, I found that the quote was true. One can certainly overdo as well as underdo giving attention to the devil. It is always worth remembering C. S. Lewis' wonderfully balanced statement in the preface to *The*

---

[1] The warfare was that which was going on in my head, not in the lack of response of the people, who were simply digesting a new kind of experience.

Screwtape Letters: "There are two equal and opposite errors into which our race can fall about the devils. One is to disbelieve in their existence. The other is to believe, and to feel an excessive and unhealthy interest in them. They themselves are equally pleased by both errors and hail a materialist or a magician with the same delight."

But it is also good to digest a less well-known quote by Lewis: "There is no neutral ground in the universe: every square inch, every split second, is claimed by God and counterclaimed by Satan."

My encounter with spiritual warfare began with a heightened awareness of the arena of this war: the Kingdom of God.

Each year I set for myself a goal of reading through the Scriptures. I'm too hyperactive to read it start to finish—four chapters of Numbers can start to drag—so I use a scheme developed by a Scottish preacher named McCheyne by which one skips around each day. On January 1, 1981, as I sat down to read, the Lord said, *Encircle the word* kingdom *every time you encounter it.* I had almost no idea what the Kingdom was, so I was eager to begin. Three months later I had read the Gospels and was astounded at the centrality of the idea of the Kingdom. But its magnitude was too great to articulate neatly, so I chewed on it from time to time over the next two years.

Then I encountered George Eldon Ladd's *The Gospel of the Kingdom.* Because I am a rather visual thinker, Ladd's chart stuck in my mind as the most reasonable overview of life on the surface of this planet.

Ladd puts us somewhere in the time slot characterized by Paul's phrase *this present evil age.* He observes that there is going to be an end to this age, focused by the Second Coming of Christ, which will escalate us to another and higher level called *the age to come.* In the age to come there will be no sin,

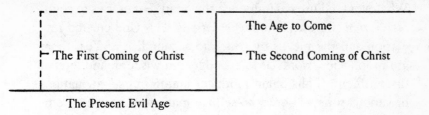

no sickness and no death. The rule of Christ will be absolute. And man will experience an end to his troubles.

The dotted line projects the rule of Christ back in time to His first coming. Jesus came announcing and demonstrating the Kingdom of God. As John Wimber states, Jesus challenged the kingdom of Satan in five arenas—sin, sickness, demons, natural disaster and death—conclusively defeating Satan in every arena. And He commissioned us to enjoy and extend His Kingdom. But we still have problems: *Some* are healed but not *all;* we gain victory over some sins but others still torment us; we strive for unity in the Body but manage to create divisions anyway. We are, that is, in the "already and the not-yet." We already taste something of the glory and power of the age to come, but we are not yet experiencing it in full. We know something of God's mercy and grace but realize that we do not yet know it all.

This time of the already and the not-yet is the zone of spiritual warfare.

What is spiritual warfare? I think it is God and Satan contending with each other on earth. The roots of spiritual warfare are found in Lucifer's decision to compete with God rather than serve Him. By this decision Satan cast himself into the enterprise of displacing God wherever and whenever possible. The primary locus for God is the human heart; therefore, the human heart is the target of Satan's activities.

Whatever God uses to influence the heart, Satan tries to counterfeit with his own spurious creations. Has God created revelation and the means by which to accomplish it? Yes, there are prophecies, words of knowledge and wisdom, and gifts of discernment. Thus Satan produces counterfeits—divinations of various sorts—in order to seduce man away from his Competitor.

To people bound by a Western worldview, there is a nonsensical prohibition of "quite harmless" activities in Deuteronomy 18. We are warned that there should be no one among us who

> practices divination or sorcery, interprets omens, engages
> in witchcraft, or casts spells, or who is a medium or
> spiritist or who consults the dead. Anyone who does
> these things is detestable to the Lord, and because of
> these detestable practices the Lord your God will drive
> out those nations before you.
>
> verses 10–12

Why are these things prohibited in such strong language? Because, in the view of Scripture, they work! And they work because their source is Satan. The people of God, therefore, are to have nothing to do with them. Paul says we are even to avoid being "yoked" with people who collaborate with Satan, for "what fellowship can light have with darkness?" (2 Corinthians 6:14). Agnes Sanford eventually refused to pray for healing for people who were engaged in the kinds of things forbidden above because they were dying. The power of God and the power of Satan won't mix without dire consequences to the person in whom they are asked to cohabit.

Much of the anemia of the Church today tracks from "perfectly reasonable and harmless" compromises with darkness.

One does not have to search long to find occult activities and anti-biblical sexuality in Christian churches.

I have noticed five major ways in which Satan attempts to attack the people of God.

Satan's First Spiritual Attack: Temptation

Temptation, of course, is the mainstay of Satan's kit bag. Temptation's point of entry is the mind. Satan has access to our thinking and is able to drop thoughts into our consciousness. It should be noted that this process is extremely subtle. It doesn't feel as though Satan is trying to influence us; it feels as though our own minds are producing our thoughts, and that's one reason for temptation's effectiveness. It feels "normal" rather than spiritual.

Satan knows us well, and knows what avenues to use with each of us. My particular weakness is quaintly indicated in Job's having made a "covenant with his eyes." One day years ago I was driving to the bank. I tell you, every good-looking woman in the city seemed to be lining the sidewalks of the street I was traveling. At stop signs, it was easy to linger "lookingly" before resuming movement. It was the same in the bank. I felt like staring at the ceiling in order to avoid looking at these women.

When I got back to my office, I dove into the sanctuary blurting out, "What am I supposed to do—wear blinders out there?" Immediately Jesus asked me three questions, all in the blink of an eye.

Was I ever successfully tempted?

"No, Lord, the Scriptures are super-clear on that. You never sinned."

Am I in you?

"Yes, Lord, the Scriptures are also clear that if I've invited You to live in me, You're in me."

Why don't you put those two together?

"Huh?" I replied dully. But soon it became evident what the Lord was saying to me: *I am in you, so when you are tempted, refer the temptation to Me and you'll have no more trouble with it.*

I began to experiment with that understanding immediately. As soon as I became aware that I was being tempted, in whatever area, I would say, "Lord, please defeat this temptation for me." Within seconds, I could feel the power of the temptation lessening. It was as though the enemy immediately began retreating from me, throwing the temptation over his shoulder at me a couple more times for spite, but having no effect. I was exhilarated.

But after a few months, I noticed that I would stall before giving the temptation to Jesus. He was there instantly when I was being tempted, but I began to pause. It was as though I would say, "Wait a minute, Lord, I'll give it to You shortly." After doing that for several weeks, I fell into sin. My tiny compromises with temptation's fire eventually got me burned.

God has given us a wonderfully assuring promise:

> No temptation has seized you except what is common to man. And God is faithful; he will not let you be tempted beyond what you can bear. But when you are tempted, he will also provide a way out so that you can stand up under it.
>
> 1 Corinthians 10:13

My "way out" is to refer the temptation to Jesus as fast as I can. In the tract *Temptation*, Dietrich Bonhoeffer's interpretation of "Lead us not into temptation" was this: In the presence of temptation, run the other way. It is the first step of capitulation to think, "I can handle this myself."

The Second Attack: Accusation

Satan is called "the accuser of our brothers" (Revelation 12:10). If he can't get you to sin, he switches tactics and begins to accuse you. He tries to make you feel guilty for having had the tempting thought. Many people who successfully resist temptation tumble readily to accusation. Part of the reason is its subtlety. It just doesn't feel as though it is the enemy talking to you. If feels like your own stuff.

What are the things the enemy accuses us of?

1. Thoughts. The enemy can put a thought in my mind, which I can choose to reject. But he then tries to disable me by accusing me for having the thought. My responsibility is to reject that thought, too. One day I had an improper thought about a woman I was looking at. So I said in my mind, "I reject that thought and refuse to entertain it." Immediately came the thought, "But I tell you that anyone who looks at a woman lustfully has already committed adultery with her in his heart" (Matthew 5:28).

I plunged into guilt and remorse, believing that it was the Lord who had spoken to me. After having this experience several times and feeling quite depraved about my thought life, I took it to the Lord.

You're not that fast, Mike, was His reply. Then, in slow motion, came the steps of James 1:14–15, "Each one is tempted when, by his own evil desire, he is dragged away and enticed. Then, after desire has conceived, it gives birth to sin; and sin, when it is full-grown, gives birth to death." First comes evil desire—then enticement—then conception—then sin. *The Lord was telling me that I couldn't get from evil desire to sin in a few seconds*, at least not *that* sin. (Anger I do in milliseconds.) I learned from this that the enemy is still quoting Scripture when it suits his intention to disable the people of God (see Matthew 4:6). My responsibility is not to let him get away with it.

2. Sins. Satan generally accuses us of sins we have already confessed. I have interviewed scores of people on this count. Virtually all of them say something like this: "I felt that, somehow, I was a special case, and even though others could confess and be forgiven, I couldn't be." In this instance, it is the subtle combination of thoughts *and* feelings that makes us believe the lie that we are not forgiven, in flat contradiction to the Word of God.

To confess your sins and then walk out of church believing that you are still guilty is to insult the sacrifice of Christ. It is throwing His blood back at Him, exclaiming, "This doesn't work for *me*." Yes, it does! Use your faith. *Decide* that you are forgiven, whether or not your mind and emotions agree with you. If you keep it up, they will agree soon enough.

3. Unworthiness. Psychologists estimate that self-talk goes on at 1,300 words per minute in our heads. Negative self-talk produces negative emotions that encourage negative behavior. "For as he thinks within himself, so he is" is the observation of Scripture (Proverbs 23:7, NAS). That's why the Bible has strong statements on the mind:

> Be transformed by the renewing of your *mind*.
>
> Romans 12:2

> But I am afraid that just as Eve was deceived by the serpent's cunning, your *minds* may somehow be led astray from your sincere and pure devotion to Christ.
>
> 2 Corinthians 11:3

For although they knew God, they neither glorified him as God nor gave thanks to him, but their *thinking* became futile and their foolish hearts were darkened.

Romans 1:21

We demolish arguments and every pretension that sets itself up against the knowledge of God, and we take captive every *thought* to make it obedient to Christ.

2 Corinthians 10:5

I have written both [letters] as reminders to stimulate you to wholesome *thinking*.

2 Peter 3:1

This translates into taking control of our minds. It means identifying and stopping negative self-talk. It means conforming our minds to what Scripture says is true of us, not what the enemy says is true.

Negative self-talk tends to start with *criticism* of self and others.[2]

"I'm no good."

"They're a bunch of snobs."

If it is unchecked, it runs to *comparing*, expressing itself in the "if only's."

"If only I could be as good as he is."

"If only I had different parents."

"If only I had as much education as she."

"If only I had a different spouse."

Complaining is the next step.

[2] I am indebted to Gloria Thompson for these ideas, presented in a volume of tape cassettes entitled "Free To Be," Part II, Vineyard Ministries International, 1985.

"It's not fair."

We say to God, "It's the mother/wife/husband/ kids You gave me." These complaints have the flavor of hopelessness. They do not motivate one to seek improvement.

The process next involves us in *compromise.*

"Oh, well, it's no big deal."

We scorn our former dreams and standards of ethics and morals.

"Life is just the pits."

We give in to others: "Oh, whatever you think."

Finally, the self-talk *controls* us through our culture, our feelings, our history, our roles, our associates and our negative attitudes. In extremis, the result is that we are *cut off.* We become nonpersons, cut off from life. We give up on learning, living and developing.

"Who cares?" is the summary statement, and relentless depression is the summary status.

This mindset will destroy us. Its author is Satan, who hates us. Using negative self-talk he seeks to program us, control us and steal our ministries, our relationships and even our lives.

It's clear from scientific experiments that negative thought produces a chemical change in the brain, which programs more negative thoughts, which reinforce the chemistry, which solidifies the depressed thinking—the rut gets deeper and deeper.

Most persons who suffer from depression, anger, fear and poor self-image think of themselves as victims, and so they are. But they are also collaborators with Satan. In warfare, one who collaborates with the enemy is a traitor. The right word to use is *sin.* It is a sin to agree with our enemy's accusations of us. It is sin to let him take us out of God's action by believing his lies.

When we find ourselves caught up in the cycle of negative self-talk, we must do what we do with all sin: repent. We must deliberately move from fear to faith. We must put on the new self (Colossians 3:8–10), and actualize who God says we are by choosing to speak the truth to ourselves.

I *acknowledge* who I am.

> "I am a child of God."
>
> "God has a good plan for my life."
>
> "I have the full heritage of the Son of God."

I *accept* myself.

> "I embrace my heritage, my personhood, my uniqueness."

I give *approval* to myself saying, almost as if Jesus were talking:

> "Mike, I approve of you. I approve of your uniqueness. I like the way you look, sound, think, laugh and comb your hair."

I *appreciate* myself.

> "God has done a splendid job of creating, re-deeming and sanctifying me. I stand in awe of His handiwork in me. Just look at the wonders He has accomplished in me and through me! I'm excited about the visions and dreams He has yet to unfold in my life."

I express *affection* toward myself.

> "Mike, I like you."

I *receive affection* from others.

> It's being kind to yourself, being tender and patient, allowing others to touch you and care for you.

I *affirm* myself.

> "I affirm that I am a first-rate child of God. I affirm that my old history died with Jesus on the

cross and I have been raised to a new life of grace.
I affirm that God has the very best in store for me,
and I am excited about how He is going to lead
me into it."

I take *action*.

"I have decided to move ahead and live life to
its fullest. I am going to take responsibility for my
thinking, conforming it to what Scripture says is
true of me. I will continue to update my subcon-
scious mind, tossing out the lies that have controlled me and agreeing to the truth that God
promises will set me free."

Finally, accusation is a common experience of people who
are in the process of ministry. This is what was occurring in
the event with which I began this chapter. Just when God is
poised to heal someone, I have often had the most distressing
thoughts enter my mind. At first I retired quickly from the
awaited healing, leaving the person sick and secluding myself
in a cocoon of self-condemnation. Later I learned to postpone
the self-condemnation, putting it off until the ministry was
finished. Finally I saw the self-loathing as a desperate ploy of
Satan to sabotage the healing.

Today when this phenomenon occurs I rebuke it and go
right on ministering. Sometimes I take a few seconds to rebuke it. But I never let it disqualify me from collaborating
with the power of God.

The Third Attack: Deception

Deception is involved in temptation and accusation, of
course. Here I am referring to deception in the matter of
doctrine. The Church has misused the issue of doctrinal purity to fight the Church rather than the enemy of the Church.

Over and over we have seen churches split over matters of doctrine. We have seen denominations rail at one another over doctrinal differences. I think I see signs that the best of the Church is repenting of that abuse.

But that doesn't mean wrong thinking is harmless. If Satan can get you to defend wrong thinking, he will soon have you defending the wrong behaving that comes from it.

I suppose a workable definition of deception is thinking you are right when you are wrong. There is in our society a re-markable assumption that our minds can produce truth on their own. Much of the Church agrees, leaving us without the tools of self-correction. The plumbline of self-correction is the Scriptures. They are the test-stone of truth. They are half of the weapon against deception, the other half being the Holy Spirit who quickens the appropriate Scriptures to counter a specific error.

The Fourth Attack: Harassment

It should be noted that the intensity of spiritual warfare ebbs and flows. Three or four times a year, our congregation comes under intensified warfare—temptation, accusation and harassment particularly. This barrage lasts two to three weeks, and then it lifts. Sometimes the attack is due to an imminent ministry trip. Because the congregation is in pretty good com-munication with itself, we quickly become aware of these times of siege. Three times in his definitive statement about spiritual warfare—Ephesians 6—Paul emphasizes that we are to "stand." Success, under spiritual attack, is standing your ground, refusing to be pushed around.

Harassment is a catch-all category of irritations. It includes these factors:

- Fatigue—the sudden onslaught of fatigue, especially when one is scheduled to attend an important meeting.
- Irritability—grouchiness. Having to bite the tongue to keep from speaking sharply.
- Miscommunication—misinterpreting simple communications between close associates or family members.
- Getting sick—you or someone close to you coming down with symptoms that threaten the accomplishment of something for God.
- Mechanical failures—cars breaking down, appliances going on the fritz.
- Attack—within days of going on ministry trips, these are some of the things that have happened to my family when I have forgotten to put protection on them: my wife barely missed being hit by a drunk driver; my oldest son was robbed at knifepoint; my second son was beaten at school, his finger was cut off and he was bitten in the back by a dog that jumped a seven-foot fence; my third son fell on broken glass causing $2,000 worth of hand surgery; my fourth son had a serious bike accident, putting him in the hospital for several days, and his sleeping bag caught on fire in a cabin. So I try not to forget protection anymore.

The Fifth Attack: Demonization

Due to space limitations only the briefest reference can be made here to this area of attack. I mention it here only to fill out the list of ways in which Satan seeks to influence mankind. I would add only that Christians are not exempt from the possibility of demonic influence. It's a nice idea that "Christians cannot have demons," but the testimony of Scripture and the Church is that they can.

Protection

If it is true that the Kingdom of God is constantly contesting with the kingdom of Satan; if it is true that the nature of spiritual warfare is attack and counterattack; if it is true that Christians have been conscripted into the army of the Lord; if it is true that the weapons of spiritual warfare are not the same as the world's weapons, then Christians must learn to take seriously the matter of spiritual armament. I have chosen to write about this by means of sharing a prayer, some version of which I say each day:

> Lord Jesus Christ, I greet You this morning as my Commander and Chief, reporting for duty. But first, I need to clothe myself and ask You to cover my family with Your armament, for my own is of no use against the enemy. Therefore, I take to myself the belt of truth. I will desire, speak and act in accordance with the truth. Second, I take on the breastplate of righteousness. Thank You that this is Your righteousness, and that it protects my vital organs, especially my heart. I will speak, think and act righteously. Third, I put on the shoes of the Gospel of peace, and I will prepare that Good News by reading Your Word and by being ready to give an account for the hope that is in me. Fourth, I take on the helmet of salvation. Save me, Lord, from the world, the flesh and the devil. And I will trust You to give me the mind of Christ and to think Your thoughts in my mind. Next, I take the shield of faith by which to quench all the flaming arrows of the enemy—arrows of temptation, accusation, deception and harassment. Finally, having seen to my defense, I take the sword, that particular Word that the Spirit gives, to utter against Satan in whichever way You lead. Over it all, Lord, I

take the mantle of love, asking You to give me Your love
for all whom I encounter today. I decide by this that I am
effectively armored for whatever spiritual warfare comes
my way today.

Before learning to do this, I was compelled to rise from my
work and go outside to check on my kids if I heard car tires
screeching to a halt. Fear would not let me continue until I had
satisfied myself that they were O.K. After learning how to avail
myself and my family of the Lord's protection, I never get panicky about my loved ones, unless I have forgotten to invest us
with protection. Sometimes people challenge me on the need
to do this *daily*. But I asked the Lord about it and He seemed
to say we should put on protection as often as we get dressed.

Periodically, the Lord lays a responsibility on me to put
protection on a person or group. Every one of the 444 days our
people were hostage in Tehran, I prayed for them, and was
delighted when they were all returned unharmed, at least
physically. The day President Reagan was shot and the day
the Pope was shot were days I had forgotten to pray for them.
I'm not the only person who prays for them, obviously, but it
would not surprise me if a critical mass of those who do had
somehow been hindered from doing so on those days.

Vulnerability to spiritual warfare means being open to its
reality. It means agreeing with what Scripture says about the
devil. It means overcoming our worldview blockages and doing what some would call "silly things," such as telling fear to
get off your back.

The next chapter deals with another experience we would
often like to avoid, that of obtaining guidance. When finitude
tries to collaborate with infinitude, there is a considerable gap
that guidance has to bridge. It is fascinating to see what God
has done to bridge the gap and truly speak to His people.

8
Vulnerability to Guidance

In the last chapter we looked at what we can do to deal effectively with our enemy. In this chapter, we find there is Someone with whom it can seem almost as difficult to deal, because we do not readily understand how He communicates with us. Just as dealing with Satan can be complicated, learning to hear God can be complex also. The process starts with being vulnerable to the knowledge that God *wants* to communicate with us.

For the first two years after I was spiritually renewed in 1972, I asked the Lord almost daily for guidance. Nothing much seemed to happen. I knew that I needed guidance badly, but my cries seemed to go unanswered. Finally I got angry about it, telling the Lord, "I'm sick and tired of asking for guidance all the time and Your doing nothing about it. From now on, I'm not asking anymore, I'm just insisting that You guide me."

Funny thing was, I started getting guidance. Faith is not so much a matter of pleading with God as of *deciding* that He is answering. My anger got me past pleading and into deciding.

Some time later, I had a sudden revelation that I should put faith in God's ability to speak to me, not in my ability to hear Him. When I put faith in His ability to speak to me, my focus is on the right area—Him!—but when I put faith in my ability to hear Him, my focus is on the wrong area—me. God knows everything there is to know about me. He understands my history, the peculiarities of my thinking processes, all the books I have read and my momentary openness or closedness to Him. So He knows how, when, where and through what particular words or images or memories or thought patterns or people or events to speak to me.

Over the years, I began noticing some patterns in His speaking to me that I would like to share.

One of the most valuable things I have learned is what I call the "confirmatory principle of guidance." Since the business of collaborating with God involves variables such as finitude and infinitude, spirit and mind, human weakness and divine power, it seems that God has decided to counteract the variableness with several factors that confirm one another when it comes to hearing Him. In relatively minor matters, less confirmation is needed than in major ones.

The factors He uses to confirm each other are these: Scripture, one's spirit bearing witness, circumstances and the discernment of mature persons in the Body. When these four all line up, one can be pretty certain that God is leading in major matters. In minor matters, it seems that two of them are sufficient, that is, Scripture and spirit. Let's take a look at each of these elements as they pertain to guidance.

Scripture

Scripture seems to be used for guidance in two ways. First, it is a check against misdirection. If the thought comes to mind *Go to the local market and steal food and give it to the poor,*

one checks Scripture and remembers, "Thou shalt not steal."
The thought was not from God. God's speaking today is not
going to contradict God's speaking in the Scriptures.

There are, however, many situations on which the prohib-
itive nature of Scripture is silent or unclear. I have observed
Christian leaders in church and parachurch organizations finding that members practice the ministry of inner healing and
expelling them because that ministry is nowhere mentioned
by that name in Scripture. This is why, I think, the Lord uses
several means to confirm His leadings.

A second use of Scripture comes when the Spirit quickens
or reminds us of a passage or puts a reference in our minds. I
described such an event in chapter 5, when the Lord quick-
ened the verse "Owe no man any thing . . ." to Sue and me.
The Lord has access to our intellects and He can drop a piece
of data into our minds. Often that data is from Scripture.

Sometimes Scripture seconds a contemplated course of action; sometimes it initiates it. The episode in chapter 5 was
confirmatory. On another occasion, it came to my mind to
read Ezekiel 37. The message from that chapter was that a
stick called *Judah* and another stick called *Ephraim* were to be
joined to become one stick. Then the Lord spoke encourag-
ingly to me about joining my church with another for mutual
encouragement and cross-fertilization. That joining is still taking place.

We cannot recall the whole Bible at any one moment. But
the Spirit knows the whole thing, and can be relied upon to
put His finger on relevant passages when it suits the needs of
guidance.

One's Spirit Bearing Witness

First John 2:20 claims, "But you have an anointing from the
Holy One, and all of you know the truth." As a pastor who has
seen people go off the beam, becoming agitated over what

they considered "an anointing," I can shudder as I read these words. I wish these people had used the second principle of guidance that came to my attention years ago when I was having the wheels of my car spin-balanced. In those days, they had to perform that maneuver with the wheels on the car. The mechanic jacked up the rear end, attached a balancing mechanism to the hub of the right rear wheel, and had his helper run the engine up to an appropriate speed. As the wheels spun, he put his left hand on the fender over the tire, extending his pointer finger upward.

I could see immediately that the wheel was off-balance. The mechanic's finger shook violently as the engine reached cruising speed. Then, the mechanic's right hand making a series of adjustments with the mechanism on the hub, his finger shook less and less until it was still. He ordered the engine stopped. The mechanism told him where to put weights, which he placed on the wheel, finishing the job.

As I watched, the Lord told me that guidance is like spin-balancing. When my plans are not in balance with His plans I become agitated, just as the mechanic's finger was agitated. "Let the peace of Christ rule in your hearts," says Colossians 3:15. Christ's peace is experienced as stillness, and unpeace is experienced as agitation.

Over the next few months I began to experiment with peace. Some opportunity would come up, for example, and I would say, "Lord, I think You want me to do it." Then I would wait and see what peace I had or didn't have. I would either feel stillness (often in the area beneath my breastbone) or feel agitation, which I interpreted as unpeace. Peace was "yes," unpeace was "no."

Peace seemed to be a valid and deciding factor. A priest from a neighboring diocese, for example, called to ask if I would lead a retreat for the clergy of that diocese. It seemed

like a God-arranged circumstance, the Word certainly sup-
ported the idea, but I had a schedule conflict. I'd committed
myself to a week-long prayer gathering. I had no leadership
role at the prayer gathering and the event could get along
perfectly well without me, but . . . .

"Lord," I said, "I think You want me to do that clergy
retreat." Pause. Then agitation occurred beneath my ster-
num. "Oh, no," I groaned, "You are saying no?" Then, to
countercheck it, I said it the other way. "O.K., You're saying
I should not do the clergy retreat." Pause. Then stillness took
the place of the agitation.

What I have found is that the Lord has an opinion on everything I propose to do. That opinion comes in response to
my statements. Whatever statement I make about a proposed
course of action He will respond to. Stillness—peace—is His
agreement with the statement; agitation—unpeace—is His
disagreement with it.

Having told the priest who issued the invitation that I
wasn't allowed to accept, I went to the prayer gathering. I
have to admit that I went not too happily. But that prayer
conference changed my prayer life. It was more important for
my prayer life to be changed than to lead those clergy through
a retreat.

There have been a few times when I could not discern
peace or unpeace. In those circumstances, I have found that:
a) either course of action was acceptable, or b) I hadn't yet
made a statement the Lord wanted to answer, in which case
it was necessary to listen for clarification.

To support or challenge this practice, I did a word study of
Colossians 3:15, "Let the peace of Christ rule in your hearts."
Peace is the gift of the risen Christ, who is the Prince of Peace
and gives a peace the world cannot give. *Heart* is the word
used for the human spirit, the core identity; it is almost never

used to describe emotions. *Rule* is the Greek word *brabeueto*. This is the only place it occurs in the New Testament. Its literal meaning is "umpire," which is wonderfully felicitous, for umpires are noted by one distinguishing characteristic: They never equivocate. The pitch is a ball or a strike, but it is never both at once. The runner is safe or out, but not something in-between.

The distinction between having peace in the spirit and in the emotions is important to understand. There have been numerous times when I perceived peace in my *heart* although my *emotions* were upset. Once our son Jason was missing from a weekend retreat. Should we initiate a police search? No. My emotions were in an uproar but my spirit was at peace. Sure enough, Jason was safe with a friend. Sue and I rejoiced not only because Jason was safe but also because God had given us His guiding peace.

If we had not been open to receive His guidance we would have run around doing all sorts of agitated things.

I have never found that I can manipulate the peace. It's there or it isn't, and I cannot make it be there or not be there. This makes peace of inestimable value, for I can influence my reading of Scripture and I can engineer circumstances and I can sway other people, but I cannot manipulate my spirit. I see why the Lord says peace is to rule.

Circumstances

When God guides through circumstances, He tends to open or close doors. We should have no control over the circumstances. I never engineer an invitation to do a speaking engagement, for example, preferring that the Lord set up the occasion through other people.

God is ceaselessly at work producing specific outcomes. He

has chosen to work through people to further His purposes and will guide us into His work, often using circumstances. Often the circumstances He engineers are, when one thinks about them, quite reasonable. But there are those strange times when people feel guided to put their hands to projects the rest of us think chancy or a waste of resources. A couple in our congregation received an unexpected invitation to teach in a small school in Damascus. After looking at other signs of His guidance they agreed that this circumstance was indeed God at work. They have just concluded two wonderfully fruitful years there.

Mature Advice

The fourth factor in getting guidance on major matters is the concurrence of mature people in the Body of Christ. None of us is sufficient alone. There are perspectives that it never occurs to me to entertain. Another's mature insight may be exactly what propels me toward a godly decision or diverts me from a mistake. Over and over I have seen career decisions announced *after* the fact, when input from others is too late. The same God who constructs us as different parts of the same Body is the God who inspired the wisdom of Proverbs 15:22: "Plans fail for lack of counsel, but with many advisers they succeed."

When contemplating a major decision, it is a good idea to seek the input of people of like mind to you: friends, associates and supporters. But I would encourage you also to be open to advice from someone who is normally not a confidant, but whose integrity you respect.

Confirmatory Dynamics

Circumstances can seem to propel us to quick decisions, but I would enjoin you to take your time until all the factors line up. When the vestry of my current church issued the invitation to me to be their rector, I took a full month to make up my mind. The norm is a few days, perhaps a week at most. But I was no way near ready to accept in a week. Even if it were God's will for me to accept, to do so without the security of the several factors coming into agreement would have thrown me into uncertainty if difficulties should later emerge. If God knows that I have to make a decision by such and such a date, He can simply back up in time and initiate the process earlier so that I have sufficient time to make a confirmed decision.

A confirmed decision is one in which the four factors we have discussed come into alignment. In major matters three out of four is not enough. Our faith is that God is at work in all four, and will use all of them to confirm and give assurance that the decision is right. It should be realized that Satan can counterfeit three of the four: He can misquote Scripture (as in Jesus' temptation), he can affect some circumstances and he can influence the advice of others. But Satan cannot touch the peace in your spirit. He can indirectly influence your peace by leading you into sin. He can affect your emotions and your mind. But if you are walking with Jesus, Satan cannot affect your peace.

There is some teaching running 'round the Church that God is eager to give us our heart's desires. I think that is true because, ultimately, the good He wants to give us is our deepest desire. My problem is that I know my heart so poorly I cannot recognize His best for me. Once, in prayer, it occurred to me to ask the Lord if I needed a confessor for a while—which, in our church, is a priest who regularly hears your confession of sins.

Yes, came the answer.

"Who should it be?" I asked.

He told me.

"You're kidding!" I reacted. He was very traditionalist and

I had heard that he thought that the charismatic renewal of which I was a part was ruining churches. I wasn't eager to expose my sins to his scrutiny.

But it was useless; I had been spoken to. When I checked it with my spirit, I had peace. So, for a year, I went to this priest for monthly confession. It was both terrible and wonderful. The terrible part was having to disclose just how rotten I was. The wonderful part was receiving assurance of forgiveness through this man—as well as acceptance from him instead of the rejection I had feared.

The Word of Knowledge

Almost all of the things that God has spoken to me have involved the use of what 1 Corinthians 12:8 (KJV) calls "the word of knowledge." The word of knowledge is a gift of information from God that the receiving person could not obtain by human means. Sometimes someone *else* has been the receiver of a word of knowledge, relaying it to me. In a gathering of clergy some years ago, a pastor I did not know asked if he could tell me something he felt was from the Lord. The core of his knowledge about me was that I had been suffering from fear. That was true. He also knew that the Lord had freed me from the fear. And he said that I would go forward no longer hamstrung by that fear. It was a great blessing to have that assurance delivered in this fashion.

Spiritual gifts such as the word of knowledge are not magic. To operate in them, in fact, feels entirely normal. They are a commingling of the natural and the divine in which it is difficult to state which part is natural and which part is divine. Many people, when speaking in tongues for the first time, for example, are disappointed that the experience isn't more "electric." Alternately, they doubt that it was the Spirit at all because it felt so normal.[1] The word of knowledge is like that. Its operation feels completely normal, and it is only by the results that someone knows for sure that he received such a word.

In the Bible we see the word of knowledge operating to meet several needs. In a number of instances it was used to reveal sin.[2] Sometimes it helped someone find something that had been lost.[3] It could warn in order to provide safety.[4] It revealed thoughts[5] and often provided direction by which another gift, healing, might occur.[6]

When I first discovered John Wimber's healing model several years ago, I took a team from our church to another town where some of Wimber's people were teaching. Someone asked if our team would pray for a surgeon who had arthritis in his hands and wrists. As I interviewed him, asking how long he had had the condition, I tried to be open to anything the Lord might have to say. The idea of bitterness came to mind. It was so slight that I almost dismissed it. Besides, I had heard infantile teaching that held that bitterness was always the source of arthritis, which I knew was foolish. But the thought had lightly wafted through my mind, and I had nothing else to go on, so I asked him if there might be any bitterness in his past. Before he could answer, I said more: "Might you be bitter at some former business partners you think cheated you when the business dissolved?"

"Yes!" he said.

---

[1] In addition, of course, the devil is fast at work to tell the person through his thinking and/or emotions that he has just made it up and that it's not by the Spirit that he is doing it.

[2] Nathan to David, 2 Samuel 12:1–7; Elisha to Gehazi, 2 Kings 5:20–27; Jesus to the woman at the well, John 4:17; Peter to Ananias, Acts 5:1–6.

[3] Samuel giving a word of knowledge to Saul, 1 Samuel 9:20, 10:22.

[4] Elisha to the king of Israel, 2 Kings 6:9.

[5] Jesus to the Scribes, Matthew 9:3–4.

[6] Jesus and the paralytic, Matthew 9:2; Jesus and the Roman official, John 4:50; Jesus and the man ill for 38 years, John 5:6.

"Why don't you make that right with the Lord while we wait," I said. And he bowed his head, silently getting the matter squared around. When he finished, I took his right hand in mine and began to pray. Over the next ten minutes the team and I prayed for him three times. At first the pain went away. We prayed again. Then mobility was restored. We prayed again. Finally, strength came to his wrists and hands again. So the word of knowledge had been used to achieve healing.

How does the word of knowledge come? Something like this. A TV signal does not come directly to the screen. It has to go first to the receiver, which translates it into pictures and sounds. Since the human spirit is the site of the presence of the Holy Spirit, it is reasonable that it is the spirit to which the Spirit speaks. We would dearly love for Him to speak directly to the mind, but He doesn't seem inclined to do that. He speaks to the spirit instead.

Space scientists have to propel a rocket through a window in both space and time in order to achieve the proper orbit. The trick, by analogy, is for us to open a window between the spirit and the mind, so that the Lord can bring data from the spirit into the mind. How to open the window? I find it works best if I relax. Our society finds it hard to think of relaxation as a key to successful work, but there it is. How to relax? Well, you can quiet the mental processes, stop thinking so intently. It helps to shrug your shoulders and relax physically. If you pray in the Spirit, do so. All the while, pay attention to the impressions that come to mind from your spirit.

These impressions are slight. As I mentioned in chapter 3, God speaks in a "whis," which is half a whisper. It is not dramatic, but it is His style. Remember that He spoke to Elijah on Mt. Horeb not in the dramatic things—rock-shattering wind, earthquake or fire—but in a "gentle whisper." These are the ways that gentle whisper comes:

- *Pictures.* One will "see" images that flash across the imagination. Sometimes these pictures are so slight that one sees them, as it were, on the after-image of the inner eye.
- *A picture of a word.* At various times I have seen words spelled out.
- *A rush of compassion.* Here, the window is between the spirit and the emotions. Some people feel compassion well up in them toward a particular person. It often signals that the Lord is going to heal the person.
- *A pain in the body.* Here, the window is between the spirit and the body. For a few moments, one feels in his own body someone else's pain as a signal that God wants to heal.
- *An impression.* This is simply an impression, often vague, that such and such is the case.
- *A concept.* Some people do not think visually. In their case, the word of knowledge comes as a concept.
- *A memory.* The memory will be of something that happened to you or someone you know.
- *A common-sense observation.* This is how the word of knowledge comes to my wife. She doesn't usually get pictures and impressions. She just looks at the person and thinks what the obvious thing is that he needs. But the person receiving the observation often takes it as from the Lord because it is so appropriate.
- *Words forming spontaneously on your lips as you utter them.* You hear the words at the same time others do, therefore having no ability to monitor them.
- *Hearing a word.* Sometimes I will "hear" a word somewhere in my mind.

I want to restate that these impressions feel entirely normal. They will work in concert with, rather than in opposition to, the person you are in the natural. If you visualize a lot, that's probably how the word of knowledge will come. If you

conceptualize, it will come as concepts. Do not imitate someone else or you will end up frustrated and confused.

Risk is an unavoidable factor in using any spiritual gift,
including the word of knowledge. *The only way you know if the
word you may be getting is valid is to express and take action on it,*
provided such action is scriptural. It is exceedingly rare for
God to authenticate the truth of the word before using it;
therefore, it is wise to be humble. Consider these two ap-
proaches: "God has told me that you are a liar and that is why
you aren't healed. So repent!" Or, "The idea of lying has
come to mind; could it be that you have a problem in this
area?" Do you hear the difference between those two ap-
proaches? Don't make the risk-taking nature of using the word
of knowledge riskier than it already has to be.

It often feels emotionally as though you are lying when you
give a word of knowledge. The enemy influences your
thoughts with self-talk and your emotions with discomfort to
attempt to dissuade you from using a word of knowledge. But
it is a gift of incalculable value—pinpointing causes of problems, dramatically shortening the time needed to solve problems, providing the needed next step when there are many
possibilities to choose from, and communicating what is on
God's heart for a person, group or situation.

Each Sunday there are about sixteen people scheduled to
minister to the needs of people in our church. Just before the
time of ministry, we wait to receive and pass on words of
knowledge. On average, there will be ten to twenty such
words. The effect of hearing one's problem or sickness la-
beled, at God's initiation, is to rise in faith that He will meet
the need. And then He does.

God is willing to guide. If we are willing to come into
alignment with His methods, we can be assured of growing in
vulnerability to guidance and therefore in usefulness to Him
as He builds His Kingdom.

9
Vulnerability to God's "Collective" View of His People

One of the most difficult biblical concepts to grasp—much less to accept—is that God thinks of us in two ways: first as individuals, with personal responsibility; but also as a community, with corporate responsibility.

This is hard for people with the Western worldview even to *look* at without getting upset and shouting, "Foul!" I will make a guess. A little further in this chapter you will say to yourself, "That's unfair!" But I urge you to keep reading. Open yourself—become vulnerable—to an idea that is thoroughly Bible-centered. Also, don't lose sight of the fact that we all *benefit* from being mystically tied to the past and to those who came before us.

Here is how this disturbing and wonderful realization first came to my attention. Several years ago I began noticing in the Bible that people had good and bad effects on others, whether those others wanted to be affected or not. I am not referring to such obvious examples as war, in which a conquering army has an effect on the conquered, but on more subtle matters. If we look at a number of passages, what I am getting at will start to be clarified.

Second Samuel 21 tells a typical story to illustrate the "dynamic of communality," as I call it. For three successive years there was famine, "so David sought the face of the Lord. The Lord said, 'It is on account of Saul and his blood-stained house; it is because he put the Gibeonites to death'" (verse 1). David's response was to call the Gibeonites to ask what they needed in order to be avenged. He added, "How shall I make amends so that you will bless the Lord's inheritance?" (verse 3). Their answer: "As for the man who destroyed us and plotted against us so that we have been decimated and have no place anywhere in Israel, let seven of his male descendants be given to us to be killed and exposed before the Lord at Gibeah of Saul" (verses 5–6). David agreed, and seven of Saul's sons died. Verse 14 concludes, "After that, God answered prayer in behalf of the land."

The dynamic of communality played out in several ways. First, the people were suffering for what Saul had done to the Gibeonites. Was it their fault that Saul had sinned? No, but they were suffering anyway. Note that God was the author of their suffering, being the One who withheld the harvests. Second, David was aware that something was wrong and searched for the cause. Finding it, he could have said, "Well, that's not *my* guilt, so there's nothing I can do." Instead, he assumed that he bore responsibility, and that he had to make things right. Third, when he addressed the Gibeonites, he acknowledged that he needed their blessing. Fourth, the seven guiltless sons of Saul were put to death for their father's sin simply because they were his sons. God seemed to think this was proper, for He then "answered prayer in behalf of the land."

Another example occurs three chapters later, this one more complex and seemingly unfair. Second Samuel 24 starts, "Again the anger of the Lord burned against Israel, and he incited David against them, saying, 'Go and count Israel and

Judah.' " Note that it is God who told David to count the people, because of their sins. The story gets complicated because Joab exhorted the king not to do "such a thing" since God had apparently forbidden the taking of a census. But David prevailed and the headcount was taken. Verse 10: "David was conscience-stricken after he had counted the fighting men, and he said to the Lord, 'I have sinned greatly in what I have done. Now, O Lord, I beg you, take away the guilt of your servant. I have done a very foolish thing.' "

Next thing: God told David's seer, Gad, to deliver three options by which punishment was to be carried out: three years of famine, three months of being chased by enemies or three days of plague. David opted for the quick way, and in the next three days seventy thousand Israelites died. David lamented, saying, "I am the one who has sinned and done wrong. These are but sheep. What have they done? Let your hand fall upon me and my family" (verse 17). Gad told David to get Araunah's threshing floor, build an altar and make sacrifices, which he did. "Then the Lord answered prayer in behalf of the land, and the plague on Israel was stopped" (verse 25).

Let's recap: God tells David, as a general policy, not to take censuses. But the people's sins incite the Lord's anger against them, and He tells David in this particular instance to take the census. David does. Then David repents. Doesn't this seem strange? *We* would not likely repent of something God had explicitly told us to do. If evil resulted, our attitude would be, "Let the chips fall where they may, I was just following orders." But David's attitude is to repent. Having a reason now—David's sin—to afflict the people, God sends a plague, at David's choice. Staggering masses die. Is it likely that only those seventy thousand had sinned? I think not. I imagine there were numerous children who died: such is the nature of plague. David's prayer acknowledges that those dying "are but sheep. What have they done?" David makes the sacrifices that have been directed and the plague stops.

This look at God is almost impossible for us in the West to accept unless we open ourselves to another worldview, namely that the *community* has a unique importance. I am coming to feel that God sees us as communal to a much greater extent than our individualistic worldview allows. It does not seem fair to us that God would cause David to sin because of the sins of the people and then punish great numbers, many of whom were not guilty, because of David's sin. But it seemed fair to God. If God held our individualistic view of persons, such a thing would have been unthinkable. But God holds His own collective view of persons, seeing us as a whole. He also sees us as individuals, of course, but *individual* does not mean separable from the whole.

The above instances are not flukes. The Scriptures are riddled with the dynamic of communality:

- Genesis 12:3, to Abraham, "All peoples on earth will be blessed through you."
- Jeremiah 10:21, "The shepherds are senseless and do not inquire of the Lord," but it is the people, not the shepherds, who "are scattered."
- Jeremiah 31:29, "The fathers have eaten sour grapes," but "the children's teeth are set on edge."
- Jeremiah 32:18, "You . . . bring the punishment for the fathers' sins into the laps of their children after them." Psychologists have demonstrated the truth of this passage, showing that abused children are far more likely to abuse their children, if this dynamic is not healed.
- Matthew 5:32, "But I tell you that anyone who divorces his wife, except for marital unfaithfulness, *causes her* to commit adultery."

- Matthew 9:2, "When Jesus saw their faith, he said to the paralytic, 'Take heart, son; your sins are forgiven.' " It wasn't the paralytic's faith that permitted the healing, but his friends'.
- Matthew 18:5, "And whoever welcomes a little child like this in my name welcomes me."
- Matthew 18:6, "But if anyone causes one of these little ones who believe in me to sin, it would be better for him to have a large millstone hung around his neck and to be drowned in the depths of the sea." The little one can sin, but he can be caused to sin, which is the greater matter.
- Matthew 25:40, "The King will reply, 'I tell you the truth, whatever you did for one of the least of these brothers of mine, you did for me.' "
- John 9:2. We see the disciples' awareness of this dynamic when they ask, "Rabbi, who sinned, this man or his parents, that he was born blind?" In this case, the dynamic was not the cause of the condition, but it was reasonable to surmise that it might have been.
- Hebrews 12:15, "See to it that no one misses the grace of God and that no bitter root grows up to cause trouble and defile many." John and Paula Sandford show with alarming clarity in *The Transformation of the Inner Man* how bitterness toward our parents can defile present people in our lives into reproducing our parents' sins against us. This is difficult for us individualists to understand, but it is a demonstrable dynamic in the lives of many. If we sin by judging our parents, we can cause others to sin against us in the same way as our parents did.

The worst and the best of the dynamic of communality is summed up in one verse, 1 Corinthians 15:22: "For as in Adam all die, so in Christ all will be made alive." You and I did not deserve to die when Adam sinned, but we did. Our spirits were snuffed out until such time as we accepted Christ as Savior. Nor did you and I deserve that Christ should die and rise for us. But He did. The fact is that Adam's sin incalculably impacted each of us personally. The greater fact is that Christ's sacrifice impacted each of us immeasurably more with present and eternal life.

If God sees us so inextricably linked with one another, and with Him, we had best see ourselves in the same way in order to collaborate with His purposes in and through us. There is an essential oneness amongst humanity. Oneness *is!* It is either positive or negative, but it already is. Unity is positive oneness; division is negative oneness. But oneness has already been achieved. It is a given. It is not a choice.

In particular, this oneness seems to extend to those with whom God sees us associated: Family? Absolutely! The poor? Yes, especially those we could help, which generally means those in our parts of the city or countryside. The nation? Yes, particularly in reference to its moral status. Other nations? How else shall this command be fulfilled, "Go into all the world and preach the good news to all creation" (Mark 16:15)?

It is important to discover with whom *God* sees us associated. I have seen well-meaning people wear themselves out trying to be associated indiscriminately with everybody. Their hearts, pocketbooks and calendars were unable to sustain that inclusiveness because it wasn't an inclusiveness determined by God. Perhaps a touch of savior-itis was motivating them.

The best place to start looking for those with whom God has appointed us to associate is in our immediate circle. He won't say, "I will put you in charge of many things" until He can say, "You have been faithful with a few things" (Matthew 25:21). I have recently experienced a radical decrease in road trips because there are relationships at home I have neglected.

How is it with your family? Are you sacrificing your own family members for the benefit of others? Do your family members feel that they have to compete with others for your attention? Do you feel that you are wasting time when you are at play with your family instead of "doing something useful" for others? Can you tell a committee at church that you cannot attend their meeting because you are taking your son to a ballgame? Oneness is not a choice. The *kind* of oneness we experience is.

Oneness is not sameness. I thank God for all the different denominations. We know that people tend to join churches composed of people like them. Thank God not every church is alike, else huge blocks of humanity would go unconverted.

Oneness is not doctrinal monochromism. Only once does the word *agree* refer to doctrine (1 Timothy 6:3). The rest of the time, agreement refers to the attitude—esteem, respect, honor—in which we hold one another. The Lord seems relatively unconcerned that we all hold the same beliefs about everything. The very nature of belief makes such agreement unlikely, even undesirable. But He is very concerned that we love each other. I looked up the word *command*. It occurs fifteen times in the New Testament. Thirteen of those times the command is to "love one another."

Oneness is not hierarchical submission. It is not subsuming one's own opinions under another's for the sake of unity. Rather, oneness is sharing convictions with superiors and subordinates and inviting them to share theirs, trusting that the real Head of the Church can pull things together.

Oneness is not cultural conformity. It is celebrating one's own culture and those of others without guilt or judgment.

Oneness is, supremely, a matter of attitude. It is a mindset and a heartset that we are all under God. Jesus holds some of His most scathing condemnations for me if I see your need and do nothing. He says that anyone in need is He. To ignore you is to ignore Him and also myself. I am not whole until you are whole. What good is it to seek my wholeness if yours goes untended? I might as well clean my fingernails while ignoring the abscess on my side. I will lose even what I think I have, for what good are clean fingernails in a body that has been killed by its abscess?

Oneness is understanding. It is the awareness that we humans are inextricably linked and that the Lord is the author of that linkage. In our congregation, this means that we make decisions in unanimity. Each person in a committee has the responsibility to ask the Lord what His decision is in each matter for which the committee is responsible. If even one member believes that Jesus is saying no to a given matter, then we pause until we come to unanimity. Fifty-one percent democracy is O.K. for governments, but it is inherently divisive in the Body of Christ.

"That means that *each person* has veto power!" one fellow exclaimed to me incredulously.

"That's right," I replied.

"Then how do you ever make any progress?" he asked.

"Progress isn't our problem," I laughed. "We go at breakneck speed." I explained that our job is to trust each other to hear the Lord and have the integrity to say what we hear. More than once, God has stopped us from an unwise decision by the unpeace of a single member. When we are in unanimity, we can proceed with confidence that God has spoken and that we are fulfilling His will.

And what if someone doesn't "buy in" to the idea of unanimity? What if he misuses that policy to get his own way?

Our experience is that when he sees that we really mean it when we say we trust him, he becomes eager to merit the trust. If someone were a real bottleneck, I suppose the Lord could find means to deal with him. But we haven't had that problem in eight years of dealing this way.

Oneness is godly largeness. The Beatitudes start with the Greek word *makarios,* the root of which means "large." Thus they mean, "How large you are if you know you are spiritually impoverished, if you mourn for others, if you are meek, if you hunger for righteousness or are merciful or pure in heart or make peace."

It is interesting to note that the prayer Jesus prescribed for us contains nine first person plural references and not one first person singular reference. What does He mean when He directs us to pray, "Forgive *us our* trespasses"? Is it simply economy of speech through which He addresses a number of single individuals, exhorting each to ask for forgiveness for his own sins, or is He also giving us direction to confess one another's sins? I think the dynamic of communality gives us the exhortation to confess the sins of people who are in rebellion or who are in an ignorance that prevents them from confessing their own sins. Job was commended in superlative terms for observing this practice: "Early in the morning he would sacrifice a burnt offering for each of them, thinking, 'Perhaps my children have sinned and cursed God in their hearts.' This was Job's regular custom" (Job 1:5; for the commendations see verse 8).

On occasion I feel the Lord prompting me to pray the so-called "Jesus Prayer," which simply says, "Lord Jesus Christ, Son of God, have mercy on me, a sinner." The practice in some Orthodox monasteries of the East is to say it many times a day. If I set out to say it for thirty minutes, I find that that word *me* applies to me, Mike Flynn, for about ten minutes. Then a mysterious change occurs, and *me* starts being others. It might be someone in my congregation for a few moments before leaping to someone else. It might be a category of persons, such as the homeless, or world leaders. My understanding of intercession is that the intercessor is identified so thoroughly with the one being prayed for that the intercessor takes his place before God. The intercessor pulls down blessing on himself, but that blessing lands on the one for whom the prayer is offered.

Will we have enough largeness of heart to pray for abundant mercies to be poured out on others? Look at the famous passage on intercession-communality found in Ezekiel 22: "I looked for a man among them who would build up the wall and stand before me in the gap on behalf of the land so I would not have to destroy it, but I found none. So I will pour out my wrath on them and consume them with my fiery anger, bringing down on their own heads all they have done, declares the Sovereign Lord" (verses 30–31).

The *gap* referred to the opening in a bivouac in which sheep were penned for the night. The shepherd lay down in the opening, so that a predator or thief would have to go over him in order to attack the sheep. Should danger come, the shepherd would "stand in the gap" to defend the flock. This time the danger, God said, was from Him because justice required that He punish the people for their sins. But His mercy moved Him to look for an intercessor who would turn aside His own justified retribution. Finding no such intercessor, He was compelled to pour out the deserved punishment.

I have no doubts that whatever gains we have made in the Kingdom of God have been charged to someone's prayer "credit card." For five years my mother and sister prayed for me to be filled with the Holy Spirit, most of which time I could have cared less and would have scorned them for wasting time had I known of their prayers.

Another time a couple of years ago I became so weakened and burdened by spiritual warfare that I was desperate. Finally I recruited eighteen people who agreed to pray for me daily. Since then I have experienced a steady ascent into greater peace, effectiveness, anointing and freedom from temptation. I was a fool to have assumed before that I could make it on my own.

There is an intriguing thought in a couple of passages in the Old Testament that suggests that people corporately are five times more effective than the same people taken separately. Deuteronomy 32:30 says one man can chase a thousand, but two can put ten thousand to flight. Two together are five times more effective than apart. Leviticus 26:8 keeps the same proportion, saying that five shall chase a hundred and a hundred shall chase ten thousand. *Synergism* is the modern word for this dynamic. But *economy* also fits because it seems that you and your prayer partner can be just as effective in one-fifth of the prayer time if you swap prayer concerns. I know of prayer partners who testify that most of the burden evaporates when they pray for each other rather than for themselves.

A few years ago I became upset that some powerful factions in my denomination were promulgating practices that were clearly unbiblical. I began grousing to the Lord that perhaps I should leave the denomination. He replied, "Where would you then go?" I didn't have any serious options, and sort of popped off, "The Baptists?"

They are already us, came the reply. It seems that from God's perspective, Episcopalians and Baptists are pretty much alike: They are both His Body. They are already us, we are already them. In God's sight, we are inseparably identified with those from whom we would escape, and they with us. We are already identified with those to whom we would go and they with us. In other words, there is noplace to go. For better or worse, God has thrown in His lot with His Church—all of it.

When I realized there was noplace to go, I began to grow. God showed me that although the prophets of the Bible were sent from God with scathing messages for a rebellious people, God never told them to leave His people. Divorce was not an option. Heartbreak? Yes. Disappointment? Assuredly. Persecution? Often. But divorce? Never. Though His people often broke covenant with Him, God never broke covenant with them, nor did His representatives, the prophets. To stay with a group you are disappointed with enlarges your heart and your faith. It brings you close to the heart of God who has promised never to leave or abandon us, though our behavior may disgust Him.

Also, God seems to have a different valuation of situations than we do, again founded on the dynamic of communality. When Elijah thought that he alone was faithful to Yahweh, God said that He had kept to Himself seven thousand who had not bent the knee to Baal. God's attitude was that seven thousand was a sufficient number. If Israel's population was three million, then seven thousand was a fourth of one percent.[1] Could this be what He means when He calls us "salt," "light" and "leaven"? It takes only a small amount of salt to season a whole meal. It takes a fist-sized lightbulb to displace a whole roomful of darkness. A bit of yeast will leaven a whole loaf.

Who are you? You are a whole community of persons. You are a multilayered community of persons. You are they and they are you. So, how are you getting along?

Some of those with whom God has placed you in the dynamic of communality are people with whom you have to work out a major issue—that of authority. In the next chapter we look at this factor, which God seems to insist cannot be sidestepped.

---

[1] On that proportion, 650,000 Christians of some level of quality in God's mind might be sufficient to stop or counterbalance national sins, such as abortion on demand in this country.

10
Vulnerability to Authority

Vulnerability to God involves us quickly in vulnerability to others, as much of the foregoing has noted. When it comes to authority, it would be nice if we could just relate to God without having to mess with people. But we are destined to find Him in one another, even in a matter as fraught with the potential for abuse as authority.

The mere mention of authority, of course, puts us in frames of mind that think of "over," "under" and "sideways." It is human nature to think first of my authority over you rather than your authority over me. To subdue the flesh just a touch, therefore, let's look first at those in authority over us.

Authority Over

Are we to exercise blind, groveling obeisance to just anyone who has gotten hold of some title that puts him or her "over" us? Actually, that is not a bad question. Let's look at some passages. Near the end of 1 Corinthians, Paul offers this advice:

> You know that the household of Stephanas were the first
> converts in Achaia, and they have devoted themselves to

the service of the saints. I urge you, brothers, to submit
to such as these and to everyone who joins in the work,
and labors at it.

1 Corinthians 16:15–16

What were the characteristics that set Stephanas' household
into over-ship? To begin with, they were the first converts
there. First converts—to salvation, to renewal—display a
readiness to hear and obey God that qualifies them for respect. They have been seeking and are ready when the Lord
presents Himself to them. They already have a heart for God
and the things of God, which sets them apart. First converts
are not always first builders or first organizers, but they are
first to believe and follow Jesus.

Second, they were "devoted to the service of the saints."
The King James translates that they "addicted themselves to
the ministry of the saints." They wanted to serve their brothers more than anything else. You would not have had to cajole
them into helping you or even going the second mile for you.
They had addicted themselves to the pursuit of the well-
being of Jesus' followers. I have had the experience of submitting to someone's recommendation largely because they
had prayed for my need more than I had prayed for that need.
When someone is that service-oriented, something in us rises
up to recognize and respond to it positively.

Those who are devoted to ministering to us often see more
clearly than we what our need or opportunity is. They have
our welfare at heart. They have taken us to God in prayer and
inquired of Him for us. That quality of love is other-centered
rather than self-centered.

Third, they "labor[ed] at it," "it" being the work of the
Church. People like this family work hard at God's business.
They spend more time than others in prayer, in service, in

witnessing, in giving and in the Word, having disciplined themselves to these practices that make for growth. They can be depended upon to be there when others have lost interest. In another passage, Paul underscores this commitment to work as a characteristic of those to whom to submit: "Now we ask you, brothers, to respect those who work hard among you, who are over you in the Lord and who admonish you. Hold them in the highest regard in love because of their work" (1 Thessalonians 5:12–13). I tell you, I pay attention to what the hard workers in our church have to say. They have won my attention and respect.

The writer to the Hebrews contributes additional characteristics to those to whom we should submit. In chapter 13 verse 7 he says,

> Remember your leaders, who spoke the word of God to you. Consider the outcome of their way of life and imitate their faith.

If we continue counting from the list above, this would be item number four: Those in over-ship speak the Word of God. Some leaders just have not gotten hold of the Word of God yet. Respect them and love them and pray for them, but ignore their words because they are *their words*. But when they speak *God's Word*, listen to them and submit to them. Paul echoes this point in 1 Timothy 5:17: "The elders who direct the affairs of the church well are worthy of double honor, especially those whose work is preaching and teaching." Those who are giving what the people need—God's Word—should be heard.

Fifth, they are models: "Consider the outcome of their way of life and imitate their faith." Among people who are living the faith will be fruit available for inspection. They will show us how to minister, how to relate, how to maintain unity, how to witness, how to give, how to disciple, how to lead, how to be led, how to heal, how to serve and the like.

Sixth, they keep watch over us.

> Obey your leaders and submit to their authority. They keep watch over you as men who must give an account. Obey them so that their work will be a joy, not a burden, for that would be of no advantage to you.
>
> Hebrews 13:17

It is instructive to remember that the Greek word for *bishop* is *episcopos: epi*, "upon," and *scopos*, "to look." A bishop is literally an overseer, one who keeps watch. The analogy in the New Testament is the shepherd. If a shepherd does not keep watch, his flock is soon scattered. There is a security in knowing that those over you are keeping watch for your spiritual safety, your growth and your well-being. We are to submit to these.

Seventh and finally, they "must give an account." As a pastor, I tell you, this scares me. It is clear that God is going to hold me responsible for the condition of my flock. I am sure that He will be fair about it, not holding me accountable for things beyond my control, but He seems to think that a lot *is* in my control.

It is a joy to serve over those who "obey" me. There are some people in my flock who will say cheerfully, "How high?" if I utter, "Jump." They don't inflate me, they humble me. They drive me to my knees in order to hear God's will for them. They draw forth caring from me, for they are my sheep. They propel me to live out the faith as wholly as I can in order not to dishonor their imitation of me.

And for whatever their reasons—many of which I am sure

are truly sound and sincerely held—it is a burden to exercise oversight over those who do not obey me. Their disobedience somehow puts the finger on the worst in me: I get proud, I answer abruptly out of the flesh instead of out of prayer, I am prone to defend myself against them, I sometimes wish they would go away and become someone else's sheep, and I have to struggle to live out the simplest tenets of the faith. When that happens, of course, I become precisely the kind of leader they don't want to submit to, which justifies their disobedience in their eyes. But, oh, what might have been!

If I am to be effective, the responsibility for that effectiveness is scattered among those who pray for me, love me, endure me, forgive me, accept me and obey me. I now realize that I play a much smaller role in both my effectiveness and my ineffectiveness than I had previously imagined.

This gets us to that difficult question, What about when leaders are wrong? We have to ask, Were they wrong because they were obeyed or because they were not? It's a chicken-and-egg sort of thing, isn't it? I believe there are many church leaders who are not speaking God's Word and therefore should not be obeyed wholeheartedly. But I also believe that a significant portion of the responsibility for this must go to those under them who have not obeyed them, prayed for them or respected them and, therefore, have collaborated in their departure from the will of God.

At present, much of the Church across this nation is at loggerheads. We have gotten into power plays that resemble hostile takeovers in the business world. Intra-denominational trust is so low that unity is a distant or even unsought goal. Interdenominational cooperation has been politicized in line with social issues. And the loudly publicized rhetoric of churchmen on all sides draws the mockery of the unbeliever rather than his respect or inquiry.

What is the answer to this mess? I don't know. I don't think it is to get more secular in our understanding and use of power. I suspect that repentance by those who are inclined to repent would be the best place to start. I suspect that repentance and vulnerability before God would allow Him to get His foot back in His churches' doors. I suspect that repentance would do more to change hearts, hear God and achieve unity than any of the methods currently being tried. If you yourself are not "inclined to repent," don't recommend this to someone you think should be.

The passages used in the section above aim at leaders. Those seven characteristics could be turned into a yardstick for those in positions of responsibility:

1. Be first in line to hear what God is doing.
2. Be addicted to serving others.
3. Work hard.
4. Speak the Word of God.
5. Live the faith. Prove that it works.
6. Keep watch over your flock.[1]
7. Remember that you will have to give an account for your people.

Authority Under

I have heard it said, "You have as much authority as you're under." I think that is so. What does that mean? Well, I have had the privilege of placing myself under the authority of several people whom the Lord pointed out to me. When I was 42, for example, I said to the Lord, "Well, Lord, here I am at

---

[1] Protect them from predators and from poisonous soul-food. Feed them the Word of God. Warn them. Discipline them. Heal them. Lay down your life for them. Shear them. Get good guard dogs to tend them while you look for the next pasture.

the stage when Episcopal rectors get another degree if they're ambitious. I'm ambitious, but I can't abide the thought of sitting in the classroom for several more years." That sentiment came out of lifelong hyperactivity and a not overly padded rear end. Sitting at classroom desks was nearly the death of me.

The Lord impressed this on my mind: *How about taking the time and money that another degree would require and apprenticing yourself to someone you admire?*

"That sounds great, Lord!" I replied. And then, in a moment of unaccustomed canniness, I asked, "Whom *do* I admire, Lord?"

How about this John Wimber guy? was the thought that came to me.

So I began hanging around John and the teams involved with the Vineyard ministry. I went to conferences they led. Eventually John invited me onto a small team for a conference. I invited myself onto other teams that traveled with him. I tried out some of the things I saw him do. Those attempts provided me with a new set of questions, so I went back and spent more time around him. Gradually, some of the things that John does I became more proficient in. That is, I began to appropriate some of the authority I had placed myself under.

Another instance. At a conference in Texas, the Lord directed me to go to a workshop given by a man I had never heard of, Rick Thomas, a Catholic priest who ministers in El Paso and Juarez. He was teaching on ministry among the poor. I was so impressed with him that I went to the repeat of his workshop, I sat near him at meals, I tagged around when he was going from one building to another, and plenary sessions found us sitting side by side. Some months later, I was invited to teach a seminar in El Paso, so I asked Rick if I could be his sidekick for a few days when my event was over. He sent me a one-word letter: "Come." Over those five days I learned wonderful things from him, all of which are now operational in my congregation and in our conferences.

Isn't it interesting that Jesus did not commission us to make leaders but disciples? If we will be good disciples, we will probably be good disciple-makers. You can give only what you have received. If you receive authority from those over you, you will be able to give authority to those under you. Or put another way: Get under those who have authority and you will find people getting under you.

Unanimity

In Chapter 9 I described how, at our church, we operate under an expectation of *unanimity*. I would add here that this practice raises people to new levels of maturity and authority because it takes seriously their ability and commitment to hear and obey the Lord.

Another recommendation is that you give your authority to others. A good management practice is to give authority to the lowest levels, for those are the people who are most engaged with the facts. But you must disciple those to whom you give authority. A too-quick gift of authority can be as devastating and frustrating as too-little. If people have placed themselves under you, you are in an excellent position to pour your life into them, for they are calling forth the best from you.

By giving away your authority, you model a behavior the Lord will expect of them later on. Inversely, if you jealously guard your authority, privileges and prerogatives, your disciples will do the same to theirs. A poorly trusted disciple will likely be a poorly trusting discipler.

Imperium and Auctoritas

There are two different words for authority in Church history. The first is *imperium*, which means "the right to command," and with it comes the right to be obeyed. The other is *auctoritas*, which means "influence," and with it comes the right to be believed. Before I say more about this, we may need a comment about my particular temperament, which is one that values harmony. I find it difficult to exercise imperium because I don't want to hurt anyone's feelings. I would much rather be followed because I am a followable kind of person than because I tell someone to do something. It is hearts that I am after, and I think you win them rather than command them.

But the authority that *I* follow, Jesus, was quite free with commands. He even commanded that people give their hearts to Him. Jesus' use of imperium with His followers hastened their growth. I notice that He used it sparingly, but did not hesitate to use it when the situation called for it. He never took away His followers' right to disobey—a mistake that many in authority commit—but He made it clear what His expectations were.

People whose temperaments value competence are usually impatient with auctoritas, choosing imperium so that the job can get done. Loyalty to them may come out of fear instead of affection, which is just fine as far as they are concerned: "I don't care if you like me, just do what I tell you." These types could profit from seeing the pains that Jesus took to be believable. He frequently implored the Pharisees, for example, to let go of their fears, traditions and laws in order to believe. He strove to be a credible witness.

Perhaps a guideline for both imperialists and auctoritators

can be found in Paul's second letter to the Corinthians, a people who had given him no end of static regarding his leadership: "This is why I write these things when I am absent, that when I come I may not have to be harsh in my use of authority—the authority the Lord gave me *for building you up*, not for tearing you down" (13:10). It might come to this question: Which will build the body up? To give commands or win their cooperation? Imperialists need to be open to the possibility of winning cooperation and auctoritators need to be open to the possibility of giving followable commands.

Bob Fulton, a friend who is a Vineyard pastor, gave us a graph once during a talk on leadership. I have found it invaluable. (See below.)

The leader is seen as a constant in this graph. The four stages represent those under a leader. Some people will never go through these stages, for they are content to follow rather than lead. God bless them, they are the heart of the Church.

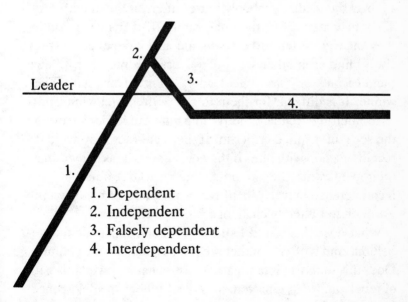

1. Dependent
2. Independent
3. Falsely dependent
4. Interdependent

But those scheduled for leadership will likely move from stage to stage.

When people come into a fellowship, they are generally at the first stage, *Dependent*. They look up to the leader. At first, the leader is wonderful in their sight, and the newcomer would defend him wholeheartedly against any attackers. If they are to progress, however, they will have to move up toward the leader-line. The leader is teaching them, modeling ministry for them, discipling them, and they are coming along. Good!

After some time under leadership—perhaps a few months with some, a couple of years with others—they edge closer to the leader-line. Now they see the leader's clay feet. They can finish his stories. They know his inadequacies. And he is just beginning to feel a slight unease about them, when suddenly—it is always suddenly—they are found at stage two, *Independent*.

The independent communicate that they can do just as good a job as the leader, probably better, if given the opportunity. They may start *taking* the opportunity. If that's not possible, they manage to find others who are also independent—they always find each other—and play "roast the preacher," "dice the deacon" or "lash the leader." They complain. They whine. It is difficult for them to stop. Often their complaints have unerring accuracy, deftly impaling the leader's flaws on the spear of inspired criticism. If they can, they may avoid direct interaction with him. If they must interact, as in meetings, their manner may be like unto a martyr who suffers another's incompetence bravely, if stiffly. Or they may throw down the gauntlet and directly challenge him in a showdown.

What does this sound like? To a leader, it sounds like rebellion. And it often is rather rebellious. But hold on a minute. Does this sound a bit familiar? Who else has followed this path of rebellion? Why, children, of course! When? In adolescence.

And that is exactly what these folk are experiencing: adolescence. The terrible side of it is all the caustic looks, the injured potential, the snippyness, the coldness, the uncomfortable scenes. The wonderful side of it is that they are growing up.

This is a dangerous stage. It is the point at which most potential leaders bail out of congregations or subgroups and go elsewhere. Some potential leaders never get into the freedoms and responsibilities of leadership because they keep exiting congregations or groups at this stage. What makes the whole thing work right, if it works right, is the maturity of the leader. That is not so unexpected. Who is supposed to be more mature, the adolescent or the parent?

The temptation is to dismiss the independents' rebelliousness. The temptation is to swoop down on them with constricting ultimatums. The temptation is to turn the matter into a war and garner supporters to your side from wherever you can find them. You may even be tempted to invite them to leave. And all the while, of course, you are certain of your justification for such actions.

But what did the Lord say to Paul in exactly this circumstance? "My grace is sufficient for you, for my power is made perfect in weakness" (2 Corinthians 12:9). And what did Paul do? "I delight in weaknesses, in insults, in hardships, in persecutions, in difficulties. For when I am weak, then I am strong" (verse 10). Jesus was saying to Paul, "Whose authority is really at stake here, yours or Mine?" As soon as Paul decided that Jesus' authority was the important thing, he could delight in the insults of the adolescent Corinthians and boast of the difficulties they presented. That enabled Jesus to show His strength more effectively.

So anyone in leadership must bite his tongue. Refuse to retort. Forgive and forgive again and yet again and again. Pray for those who insult him. Bless them who say all manner of evil against him. And wait faithfully. This is not the time to discipline; this is the time to woo, to have a generous spirit toward them. They *will* come out of it. They may have to stub their toes a few times in ministry situations, they may need to experience the full load of spiritual attack that can come to those who are out from under a leader's umbrella, they may need time to hear the Lord speak to them about their attitudes. But they will come out of this stage.

When they come out of it, they enter the transition stage of being *Falsely dependent.* By a leader's maturity, the Lord has led them into repentance for saying those things against him. He now races home from church to tell his spouse that they smiled at him in the coffee hour for the first time in months. They may think they are trying to go back to dependence, but they can never go there again. They are really trying to get back to the leader, so he must help them. He can be welcoming, be friendly, hug them and not insist on meticulous explanations of why they did what they did or felt how they felt over the last few months.

What's waiting for both the leader and the dependent is the stage of being *Interdependent,* in which they can let each other lead, as the situation requires, without that previous competition or inferiority. They are friends again. They like each other. They prefer one another in opportunity and honor. They look for ways to uphold one another. They assess one another's gifts accurately and deploy them at the nudging of the Lord Jesus.

Lateral Authority

> I plead with Euodia and I plead with Syntyche to agree with each other in the Lord.

> Philippians 4:2

Make my joy complete by being like-minded, having the
same love, being one in spirit and purpose. Do nothing
out of selfish ambition or vain conceit, but in humility
consider others better than yourselves.

Philippians 2:2–3

May the God who gives endurance and encouragement
give you a spirit of unity among yourselves as you follow
Christ Jesus, so that with one heart and mouth you may
glorify the God and Father of our Lord Jesus Christ.

Romans 15:5–6

I think there is a special application in these passages to
those who are *laterally* related to one another in the Body; not
over or under one another, but side by side. Neither submission nor dominance seems to be the issue here. If Euodia
were over Syntyche, Paul might tell her to admonish Syntyche, or he might exhort Syntyche to submit to Euodia. But
unity, not authority, is on his heart as he thinks about them.
Notice his words *I plead . . . I plead.* Paul could order them to
agree, but that probably would not work. A change of heart is
needed. So he comes as a supplicant rather than as an authority over them.

"To agree with each other." How? "In the Lord." There
are many things that can divide us, but there is only One who
can unite us. "For he himself is our peace, who has made the
two one and has destroyed the barrier, the dividing wall of
hostility" (Ephesians 2:14). Jesus died that we may be one. It
is insulting to His sacrifice, therefore, to effect division. When
we refuse to agree, to be one, to be like-minded, to have the
same purposes and goals, we slap the crucified One in the
face.

*   *   *

Being vulnerable to those in authority means realizing that they may misuse their authority. They may exhibit immaturity. They may respond to you in the flesh. They may fail to pray for you and for decisions that relate to you. They may be threatened by your abilities, gifts, anointings and experience. What then? I think the Lord wants us to submit to them anyhow both in attitude and in action. Why?

First, it builds our trust in God, who is the Author(ity) of the system. Second, it frees the Lord to straighten out the person in authority over us. When I became aware that Sue was submitting to me as the head of our family, for example, it took the Lord only two weeks to make changes in me that she had been desiring for more than a decade. Third, it frees the Lord to link us all up in His Body more intimately.

What about the vulnerability of having to exercise authority? If you use your authority, you may be misunderstood. There are those who will accuse you of being egotistical. You may be rebelled against. You may be proven to have been wrong.

Sue thinks that one of the greatest problems in the Church today is leaders who don't lead, authorities who don't author, disciplers who don't disciple. Fear is the primary immobilizer of leaders.[2] If you're immobilized, surround yourself with support, take a deep breath and plunge into leading in accordance with the best direction you can get from Jesus. But do something. Immobilized leadership immobilizes the whole Church.

Authority is loaded with dangers on both the underside and the overside. But God has organized things this way. He can make it work. Through you.

The next chapter deals with a dynamic by which we can be assured to be making the best use of authority.

[2] See chapter 3.

11
Vulnerability to the Presence of Jesus

I did not, of course, always know the things I have written about in the preceding chapters. There was a period in my life, in fact, when I was in rather desperate condition, though I probably would have denied that—one cannot admit he is in hell until he catches a glimpse of heaven. Perhaps it is time to tell you the story of how God began to get me into these things.

When I was spiritually renewed, or baptized in the Holy Spirit, I was 32 years old. I had been in the pulpit for six years and was urgently looking for a way out. I had stumbled through my first assignment for twenty months; had destroyed a second over a space of two years, after which the congregation folded; and was well on the way to messing things up again, having been in my third church for two and a half years. I wasn't evil. I was undiscipled and unempowered, but the effect on my congregations was almost the same as if I had been evil. There was tension, dissatisfaction, failure and depression—on my part and on theirs.

Not only was my professional life on the skids, but also my personal life could have been much better. There were four areas in particular that begged for change. First, I had a classic

Irish temper with a quarter-inch fuse. I was always losing my temper, with devastating results for myself and everybody else. Second, I had a good deal of anxiety. I thought it was merely the presence of conflict. I had an ulcer. Third, I was a cynic. Cynicism affected every area of my life. Even my humor had a barb in it, which I felt was justified. Fourth, I was a pornoholic. I was addicted to girlie magazines, finding myself unable to resist picking them up and unable not to sin in my heart when I had one in my possession.

What's more, I was in denial about all these things:[1] "*I* haven't failed, the churches have failed." "I have every reason to be cynical and lose my temper—just look at what a mess the world is in!" "Of course I have an ulcer—so would you if you were in my shoes." "It's only natural to look at pictures of women. It doesn't hurt anyone."

Consequently, I was planning my escape from that unworkable and fossilized institution called the local church. My escape route was by way of a discipline that was in vogue at the time, sensitivity training. I was on my way to full accreditation as a sensitivity training counselor. My plan was to make contact with people who might need my consultation skills, perhaps landing a job in my denomination somewhere or supporting my family through contacts with numerous clients. Toward that end, I was scheduled to attend a national conference of trainers in Ohio in August 1972. A couple days before the conference, I was busy fantasizing how striking, how competent, how creative people there were going to find me, when the phone rang with the message that my participation had been canceled because of overbooking.

I plummeted into depression. A door had slammed shut. I

[1] Keith Miller's book *Sin: Overcoming the Ultimate Deadly Addiction* is a classic on denial.

was held captive. I could barely stand being in a local church but I hadn't the courage to find other work. The next day was a Sunday. Somehow I got through the services, though I was feeling absolutely hopeless. Monday I went to the office, not wanting to impose my depression on my family, even though I had nothing to do because I was supposed to be out of town.

Mid-morning came a knock at my office door. I dragged myself over to it to find one of my parishioners who had been on vacation. Dully, I remembered he had been away, so I asked, "Oh, hi, Les, how was your vacation?"

"Fine," he said in an unconvincing way. Then I noticed he had something in his hand, a book. "I promised my son in Seattle that I would read this book," he said, "but I don't want to read it. Would you read it for me and tell me how to answer him?"

"What's it about?"

"Oh, it's about people who speak in tongues and stuff like that." This was said with a shrug and a grimace.

I hadn't a clue what he meant, never having heard the expression "speaking in tongues," but I wasn't prepared to acknowledge that there was something in the religious world I was ignorant about. So I agreed. Les smiled and left. I threw the book onto a corner of my desk and went on with my depression.

The next morning was Tuesday, August 22, 1972. Just as I zombied through the door, that book caught my attention as though it had been painted overnight in neon. *I might as well read this dumb book*, I said to myself, noting that I certainly had the time to do so. Settling myself into a comfortable chair, I began reading *Nine O'Clock in the Morning* by Dennis Bennett.

For the first hour or so, the primary dynamic in me was attraction-repulsion. Part of me was deeply attracted to the kind of life Bennett was describing. Another part of me—my intellect—was just as emphatically repelled, thinking—unjustly—that the book was about emotionalism, which I abhorred. One moment I would be thinking, *Oh, if only these things were real.* The next moment, *What a bunch of garbage!* Hunger and bias were fighting it out.

Meanwhile, the phone didn't ring, my secretary didn't bother me, no one came to the door and I read on.

Then something began happening in me that I can describe only by the analogy of catching a whiff of some dish that you know you like but cannot identify. As I read, the sensation grew. At some point I became aware that it had been present for a while. But as I paused, I could not identify what it was. The more I read, the stronger grew this sensation. After a timeless time, the hunger began to win out over the bias as the sensation continued. At this point, it felt like an uncontrollable, delicious tingling in my chest. I was ravenous for more.

Sometime in mid-afternoon, the tingling-hunger increased suddenly when I said in my mind, *Oh, all right. If it takes giving up my intellect in order to get some peace, I give it up.* For the next half hour, the hunger grew to an ache while the tingling rose to almost a shaking. I leaned forward, ravenous for the center of the thing I could but catch the edges of. On I pressed, not really digesting the words of the book I was reading, just ingesting them in large hunks.

Suddenly, I remembered an event that had occurred almost eight years earlier when I was in my middler year in seminary. I was deeply disillusioned with seminary and self, and made the decision to quit during the Communion service in chapel one morning. Going to the altar rail out of sheer rote, I knelt down. As the priest put the wafer in my hand, a tingling began in my insides, definitely noticeable but not alarming. I took the bread into my mouth, chewed and swallowed.

But the tingling increased as the priest came toward me with the chalice of wine. He gave the cup to the person at the end of the altar rail. As he came one person nearer to me, it increased again. By the time he was before the person next to me, the sensation had escalated to the point of distress. Had I been bolder, I would have run from the building without receiving the cup. But then, as he stepped before me and placed the cup to my lips, the worst-best happened: I was certain that my body was emitting brilliant light, which un-doubtedly was drawing the attention and scorn of my fellow seminarians.

As it turned out, no one noticed what had happened to me. So I escaped the worst. On the other hand, no one could tell me what had happened to me. So the best was undeveloped.

Now I knew what it was because Bennett had been talking about it in his book. I was being filled with the Holy Spirit—again! I knew, and I knew that I knew, that my life was changing radically at that very moment. The incredible good-ness of God! I wasn't seeking Him. I wasn't trying to grow in holiness. I wasn't even repenting of my sins. I didn't know that more of God was available to meet my needs. But He sought me out, came to me on my own turf, tantalized me with the memory of that day in seminary.

Within days, I knew that my four major personality disor-ders had been healed. Temper? I didn't even come close to losing my temper even though provocations increased. Anx-iety? The Lord gave me peace, a positive presence that felt like being full of honey. Cynicism? Why, suddenly it was as though scales had dropped from my eyes and I could see that God was good and that He was going to win. Temptation? The enemy could crook his finger at me, but I defeated his beckonings. This honeymoon, characterized by effortless-ness, went on for six months. Then the Lord removed the effortlessness and I had to start walking by faith. Meanwhile, our church became the most exciting place in the world. Within months, we were undergoing wonderful, refreshing renewal.

I was filled, additionally, with the knowledge that I was incapable of running my life. Before, I had been reasonably competent. But now I knew for a fact that if the Lord did not help me, I would blow every opportunity He sent me, I would fail every test that came to me, I would miss every directive He gave me. So I began practicing the immediate presence of Jesus.

Because I wanted Him to be Lord in every situation in which I found myself, and because a throne symbolized lordship for me, I began envisioning Jesus sitting on a throne everywhere I went. It became my habit to position Him on His throne in every room I entered. I could see Him always, usually halfway between the heads of the people and the ceiling. Often I reminded myself to look at Him. He would smile at me. I would adore Him.

To this day, this is the chief manner in which I practice His presence. This is the chief way I initiate getting words of knowledge, know what to do next, determine what to say, learn how to respond, enjoy His love.

Sometimes this becomes a roller-coaster ride. When first renewed, I began hearing the term *healing of memories*. I don't know why, but I took an instantaneous dislike to that term. My life had changed, but after all, I still didn't want to become a weirdo, and something about that term had *weirdo* written on it. So I determined to learn nothing about the ministry of healing memories. I was a bit surprised, therefore, when Agnes Sanford laid hands on me once and prayed that I would be given her "anointing" for the healing of memories.

I discounted the experience as a fluke until, a couple of weeks later, a woman came to my office in deep emotional pain.

Shortly, as I listened to her, I realized that she needed healing of a memory having to do with a rejection by her husband. I told the Lord I didn't like the idea of healing memories, but He pressed me to do it, so I said to her, "What you need is healing of memories."

"Fine," she replied. "What's that?"

Proud fellow! I wasn't prepared to tell her I didn't know, so I said, "Well, I don't have time to explain it now. Why don't we just pray?" *Oh, great!* I thought. *Now I'm going to have to deliver the goods, and I don't even know what the goods are!*

As she bowed her head, I looked at Jesus, enthroned there in my office. In my mind's eye He got down from the throne, knelt beside the woman, put His right hand around her shoulders, reached into her heart with His left hand and extracted a lump of black jello. He put the jello into His own heart, where it shrank and disappeared. Then He reached into His heart again, took out a lump of milk-white jello—the same size and shape as the black—and put it into her heart where the black had been. Then, looking at me, He said, "Do that."

Sure! was my sarcastic response. But I had nothing else to go on, so I began to pray. Over the next few minutes, it was as though a master guide took the hand of a dull schoolboy and led him successfully across a field in which were located landmines and bogs, most of which the boy never knew were there. At least six times He showed me things I had not known before; He reminded me of concepts I had not thought of for years. He dared me to identify her hurt as that ridiculous lump of black jello and His healing as that impossibly white jello. He told me to tell her that He had suffered her rejection when He was on the cross and that it had died when

He died. He promised her that the white jello represented His healing and His acceptance, which He was now giving her, and that the memory would bother her no more.

Finally, I said, "Amen." The woman reported that her emotions were healed (which later proved to be accurate). I could hardly believe it. When she left, I hoped I would never have to be that uncomfortably vulnerable again. Two weeks later, though, it was the same thing all over again. That person was healed, too. Since then, there have been innumerable episodes of healing that came about by practicing the presence of Jesus.

The remainder of this chapter is a short list of additional factors I have experienced by opening myself to His immediate Lordship.

Openness to Love

During a period when I was reading a lot about "being broken," I set a book on the nightstand, turned off the light and instantly heard Jesus say, *I'm going to break you with love.* As He spoke I was inside Him, looking at myself through His eyes.

Back in my own eyes: "But what about *these!*" I lamented, referring to my faults, which to me seemed to be pancake-sized blotches on the surface of my body.

Back in His eyes: The blotches were as tiny grains of sand, and His hand reached forth, deftly brushing them away. *There!* He said. *That takes care of that.*

"All right, Lord, I accept Your love, in spite of my flaws."

Good! He exulted, and we communed in joy.

"Love," Paul proclaims in 1 Corinthians 13, "never fails." The Greek word for *love* here is *agape*, which we understand as God's unconditional love. *Never* is *oudepote*, which is a quadruple negative having the sense of never-at-no-time-no-how. And *fail, piptei,* has the meaning of doing less than, decreasing from one level to a lower. Thus, *love never fails* means "God's love will never, at no-time, no-how do less than achieve 100 percent of its purposes."

The first response to this must be to accept God's love for ourselves. Everyone has to settle this for himself. It is scandalous, of course, that God chooses to love us exactly as we are. If I were God, I would have blowtorched me off the face of the planet thirty years ago.

Why He chooses to love me is beyond my comprehension, but *that* He chooses to love me is abundantly clear in His Word. *My job is to agree with Him.* That means willfully embracing His love and acceptance of me and extending love and acceptance to myself.

The second response is to be agents of that love toward others, or, as the imp in me loves to startle people from the pulpit, "Love the hell out of 'em! [Pause.] That's the only way the hell will leave them!" The Spanish Roman Catholics began a renewal movement in the 1940s called Cursillo—literally, short course. One of the terms they employ for *love* is "palanca," which refers to a lever. When I participated in Cursillo, people bathed me in the *agape* love of God, which gently pried loose a number of my hang-ups and sins and washed them away forever. Their love came to me as the "lever" of a crowbar.

Love never fails, but it doesn't operate with our timetable. Love says, "I'm going to love you whether or not you change." But God rewards love's immense heart and faith with eventual change in the beloved. You don't love in order to accomplish change, but as you do love, change will be accomplished.

Learning to See Him

Seeing is a central behavior in practicing the presence of Jesus. Seeing happens in two phases, which oscillate. The first is *active creation*. That is, we actively imagine the Lord and we put Him on a throne wherever we are.

Then, as we enjoy His presence by looking at Him, seeing goes into its second phase, *passive observation*. We just observe Him. *He* is the actor, if any action occurs, and we are the audience. Very often, the only action that occurs is a look of warm love.

But if He *does* something, as in that first inner healing described above, then we become co-actors with Him, and He expects us to take an active role. Sometimes this means doing a specific behavior. Sometimes it means praying in the way He guides. Thus, I "see" Him reach into the woman's heart and remove the darkness.

Trouble is, many of us try to make Jesus do what He has not indicated He wants to do. We try to create actively without having observed passively. Or we get a little cup of water and try to irrigate a whole acre, when what we need is to spend that cup on a single plant and go back to the well for more water *if* the well wants to give us more.

Sometimes you can create actively for quite a while on the basis of a direction that took but a few milliseconds to communicate.

Usually He sets a direction and asks us to check in many times as we follow that direction. It is easy to go astray. I know that I need a short tether.

Vulnerability to the Current Word

Someone once said that God is the youngest being in the universe as well as the oldest. While it is true that He is "the Ancient of Days" and "the same yesterday, today and forever," it is also true that He is always "doing a new thing." "Do you not perceive it?" is His ongoing question. God is immediately and appropriately responsive to the condition of the individual and corporate heart.

Once, after a conference where very little power had been displayed, I phoned to complain to John Wimber. John replied, "Well, remember, Mike, we're using peashooters when we need howitzers." In some parts of the Third World, you can do wonderful miracles because the level of faith is high. In much of the so-called First World, those miracles are few because the level of faith is low.

To every person and group, God has something appropriate to say. As individuals and as groups, we have a responsibility to hear the current word. What is God trying to say to you/me *now?* At any given time, God can say something that will set your course for the next five minutes or five decades. Vulnerability to the current word requires eagerness to listen and willingness to obey. It means facing contemporaneity. What's coming down *now?*

Psalm 32:9 exhorts us to be neither horse—always running ahead—nor mule—dragging its feet—because neither has any "understanding." God does not want to control us with bit and bridle, but with the still, small voice that we can hear only if we are walking in His presence, aware of when He moves and when He stops, when He turns and when He goes straight. *We* put the bits in our mouths, perceiving His tug on it in easily dismissible impressions.

Masters of practicing the presence, such as Brother Lawrence and Frank Laubach, testify that it never becomes easy to practice the Lord's presence, but that if we do it, it makes all other chores easy. We thereby get to exchange many difficult tasks for one difficult task.

What's the current word for today? There seem to be several.

First, God seems to be promising that evangelism will be significantly more productive in this final decade of the twentieth century than previously. All over the world Christians of varied hues are agreeing that this is on the heart of God.

Second, there are preparatory issues that must be addressed if evangelism is to be possible:

1. Holiness. God seems to be saying to the Church, "What are you going to bring new believers *into?*" Soporific Sardis and lukewarm Laodicea[2] are far more characteristic of the Church today than the kind of Church to which God would care to add believers. Is there any moral difference between your congregation and the world? Is your congregation noticeably more self-sacrificing, less materialistic, more righteous than the culture around it?

2. Unity. I'm not just talking about intra-congregational unity but inter-congregational and interdenominational unity. In March 1989 the pastors in my city began praying together once a week. We had all separately banged our heads against the spiritual climate of this city for many years, with no discernible change in the spiritual health of the populace. So we came together. We have found that God is cleansing us of prejudices, competition and self-aggrandizement. We care much less about the doctrinal, liturgical and historical differences among us. We just love each other and fervently pray that God will use each of us and all of us to extend His Kingdom in this place. For the first time, we have a sense in our spirits that something real is happening here.

3. Empowerment. Jesus' last will and testament to His followers was, "Do not leave Jerusalem, but wait for the gift my

---

[2] Revelation 3:1–6, 14–22.

Father promised, which you have heard me speak about. For John baptized with water, but in a few days you will be baptized with the Holy Spirit" (Acts 1:4–5). Three years of discipling, untold numbers of miracles and healings, and countless teachings and sermons were all *insufficient* to propel them into effective ministry. It is as though He said, "I don't need *your* power to do *My* work, thank you very much. You need *My power* to do *My work*, and don't put your hand to anything until you get it."

I don't care if you call yourself Pentecostal, charismatic, third-wave, second-blessed, renewed or none-of-the-above. Forget the titles, but obtain the reality. And then obtain it again and again.

4. Prayer.

Sacrificing Ourselves to Prayer

S. D. Gordon, in a moment of stunning clarity, wrote, "You can do more than pray *after* you have prayed, but you cannot do more than pray *until* you have prayed. . . . Prayer is striking the winning blow, service is gathering up the spoils." Larry Lea includes the "more" in saying that "Jesus Christ went from one place of prayer to another, working miracles in between."[3]

To say that one always practices the presence of Jesus while avoiding a specific time of prayer is like saying that one always drives the car without needing to gas up. It is interesting that the most useful servants of God are the ones who spend the most time in prayer.

Prayer looks dead-ended. And at times it is. Hudson Taylor

---

[3] Dick Eastman's book *The Hour that Changes the World* and Lea's book *Could You Not Tarry One Hour?* contain very do-able guides for spending an hour in prayer.

could say that the sun had not risen upon China for 25 years without finding him at prayer. Someone asked him how he felt when he prayed. "Nine days out of ten my heart feels like a lump of wood," was the reply. He didn't do it because it felt good, but because it was necessary.

There is a renewal of interest in prayer, which renewal itself has been borne of prayer. About twenty years ago God began putting it on people's hearts to pray for a great outpouring of prayer. The result is that there is much more prayer going on today than in the recent past.

Prayer brings us face to face with our worldview. In prayer, contrary to our worldview, we find that the spiritual is the foundation for the material. We learn to see through the material to the spiritual that underlies it. In the spiritual realm, the weapons are words. We must become conversant with those words and how they are effectively deployed in spiritual warfare. We have to ask God for the grace to pray more effectively and wait until He grants that grace, else we will set for ourselves regimens we cannot sustain.

We must come to understand what Luther meant when he said one day that he was so busy he would have to pray three hours instead of the normal two. If prayer doesn't work, that is an absurd thing to have said. If it does work, it is absurd of us not to imitate him.

People get convinced that they need to pray more before they become convinced that they must give up something in order to accomplish it. I have seen men decide to gather daily for prayer at six A.M. At the end of three weeks they are fatigued, depressed and ready to scratch the whole business. Why? Because they are still going to bed at midnight. Prayer is work. You have to make time and space and energy for it, or it will wear you out. So start small. "I am the Way" means that it is enough to be on the path; you don't have to have arrived.

In sum, practicing the presence of Jesus means spending quality time with Him regularly; it means recollecting Him habitually throughout the day; it means checking in with Him when you are faced with the need for His input; and it means holding the attitude that He is the Lord of all and that you are His servant.

To help myself keep a short tether, I bought a watch with a countdown timer. I set it for 24 minutes—one for each of the elders around the heavenly throne. At the end of that time, it beeps, and begins counting down again. At the beep, I just check in. Following Frank Laubach's tract "The Game with Minutes,"[4] I try to beat the watch by reminding myself of the Lord before the beep. It has been a blessed experiment for nearly sixteen years.

By now perhaps a question occurs to the reader: Do we ever get over being vulnerable? Since *vulnerable* has *wound* at its root, do we ever get healed of being vulnerable? The next chapter explores that question.

[4] Obtainable from New Readers Press, Box 131, Syracuse, NY 13210.

12
Meeting Our Needs through Vulnerability

At Christmas 1988, someone gave me a wall calendar decorated with quotations from C. S. Lewis, one of my favorite writers. One of the quotations has arrested my attention frequently: "Relying on God has to begin all over again each day as though nothing had yet been done." It was a timely input and it helped me realize that I would never get over being vulnerable.

In 1988, teams from my church and I conducted 22 conferences on healing. Because much good was accomplished through those conferences, it was a year of unrelenting spiritual warfare. The enemy attacked us for what we had just done and to sabotage any upcoming event. It was continuous double-dose warfare and as the leader of that ministry, I took the heaviest assault. There was temptation, accusation, illness, and in spite of prayer those attacks were somewhat successful. I ended the year fatigued, sick and feeling guilty. So I took six months off from the traveling ministry and tried to recoup.

It came to me gradually that I was lone-rangering. I was surrounded with people but I was relying on myself. Over the next few months, I tried to do something about this by calling for help from three groups. The first was a small band of lay leaders in my congregation. I met with them monthly for breakfast. I confessed my sins to them and asked them to help me achieve personal accountability. Second, I asked two other pastors to pray with me for six weekly sessions centering on my need for the healing of emotional and spiritual wounds. Third, I recruited eighteen people to pray for me daily, writing them a monthly letter updating them on what was happening.

Over the next year I experienced a gradual ascent into accountability, healing and strength. There was nothing dramatic, there were no "turning points," but I steadily got more healthy. I "lightened up." My sense of humor began expressing itself again. I began to laugh at myself again, taking myself less seriously.

But when I had to go back on the road I knew that I would come under attack again. One day I found myself sobbing because I knew in my spirit that the reprieve was over. But there was a difference. Now the attacks were neither as strong nor as relentless even though the conferences were more powerful than ever before.

Vulnerability to the Body of Christ—in those three groups—had helped me.

We may not like being vulnerable but this openness does heal. I have testified in previous chapters how I have been helped by being vulnerable to Scripture, discomfort, Jesus' worldview, Jesus' headship, self, spiritual warfare, guidance, communality, authority and the presence of Jesus. I would not take back one of these experiences of vulnerability. Though they frequently caused me various degrees of pain, they paid off so abundantly that the pain was worth it.

What's more important is that vulnerability to the things of God has benefited the Kingdom. I am expendable, but the Kingdom of God is not, which propels us into another consideration of vulnerability.

Consider Isaiah. A period of monumental vulnerability in his life is mentioned in this short passage: The Lord said to Isaiah, " 'Go, and loose the sackcloth from your loins and take off your shoes from your feet,' and he had done so, walking naked and barefoot . . . for three years" (20:2–3, RSV). The passage goes by so quickly that we can fail to grasp its implications. This man, in obedience to God, had to go around naked for three years. In Bible times nakedness equaled shame. It would be decidedly uncomfortable today—embarrassing, illegal, misunderstood—but it was scandalously shameful in those days. And that was exactly the point: "So shall the king of Assyria lead away the Egyptians captives and the Ethiopians exiles, both the young and the old, naked and barefoot, with buttocks uncovered, *to the shame of Egypt*" (verse 4).

Was it wounding to Isaiah to have to go naked for three years? Unquestionably. Did he benefit from the experience? Ah! That's the wrong question *at this level* of consideration. A whole nation was in danger of divine punishment, and Isaiah was sent as a demonstrated sermon to highlight its danger. God apparently thought an entire nation in jeopardy of being expended was worth the expenditure of one man's discomfort. For Isaiah, the issue was not benefit but obedience. Isaiah is benefiting now in heaven, of course, from his obedience, but if he had obeyed for the sake of eventual personal benefit, he would have been disappointed and his focus would have been off-course.

Look at Ezekiel. Was it wounding to be directed to lie on his left side for 390 days, bearing the sin of the house of Israel? Obviously. What do you suppose happened to his muscle tone? to his ache-quotient? to his family life? to his work? Was God aware of what it would cost Ezekiel to comply with His directives? Certainly, but He directed so anyway.

Look at Jesus. He didn't have a chance. Seven hundred

and fifty years before His birth it had already been decided that "by his wounds we are healed" (Isaiah 53:5). In fact, that particular die was cast "before the creation of the world" (1 Peter 1:20). In the Nicene Creed, Jesus' entire earthly life and ministry are summarized in the mere punctuation mark of a period: "and was made man. For our sake he was crucified. . . ." He was, in other words, born to die. He was incarnated for the purpose of being terminally wounded.

From Paul's catalog of mishaps in 2 Corinthians 6, we realize he knew what he was talking about when he said to the Colossians, "And in my flesh I complete what is lacking in Christ's afflictions for the sake of his body, that is, the church" (1:24, RSV). The message is: There is more suffering to be accomplished. Peter, likewise, exhorted his readers to accept suffering: "But if you suffer for doing good and you endure it, this is commendable before God" (1 Peter 2:20).

God is looking for people who will complete what is lacking in the sufferings of Christ, who will accept vulnerability, who will embrace costly obedience. He needs people who will sacrifice self-advancement for the sake of Kingdom-advancement. He needs people whose goal will be to reveal the image of Christ rather than achieve self-fulfillment. Does someone's self-fulfillment give Him glory? I think it does. But something has gone screwy in the Church today because gaining one's life has taken precedence over losing one's life.

When I seek to gain my life, I cannot but put my focus on me: *my* healing, *my* discipling, *my* advancing. We say that it is for the sake of the good I might do for the Kingdom of God, but something hollow results anyway. Vulnerability to God means allowing *Him* to choose the means by which His own goals in us are achieved. His *ends* focus on gain rather than loss, but His *means* focus on loss rather than on gain. "If anyone would come after me, he must deny himself and take up his cross and follow me. For whoever wants to save his life will lose it, but whoever loses his life for me will find it" (Matthew 16:24–25).

Sometimes this loss is almost laughably minor. I was invited to do a workshop at a very Protestant conference. As I was getting dressed that morning, the Lord said, *Wear the black suit and clerical collar that make you look like a Catholic priest.*

"What for?" I asked.

Because some of the people there need to see it.

"Can I tell them that You told me to wear it?"

No.

For the first half of the workshop, there were some distinctly hostile looks coming from the audience. During a break, some people gathered around the podium for conversation. One fellow, on the periphery, finally got my attention. It seems that God had used my clerical garb and my teaching to confront him with the need of reconciling with his religious past. But it would have been worth obeying directions even if there had been no noticeable benefit.

Sometimes the loss is not so minor. When I had been at St. Jude's for two years, I was walking a tightrope between trying to satisfy traditionalists in the congregation while advancing renewal. It was about that time I began taking the last Tuesday of the month for a day-long prayer day. One Tuesday, I walked to the top of the mountain behind Burbank and quickly found myself in agony of soul. Something was trying to get born in me, and I was in "labor" for about four hours: I ached over the divisions in my congregation, I agonized over my seeming inability to lead the flock into vitality and unity, I was disgusted with the wimpyness of our faith and the flaccidity of our worship. I stalked back and forth across the brow of that hill, I lay down in the dirt, I stalked again, I lay down again. I simply couldn't get comfortable in body or soul.

Finally, it was time to leave for home. In anger, I snatched up my Bible and canteen and set off for the car, two hours down the mountain trail. Just as I came off the crown of the hill, the whole day's agony erupted in a single sentence: *No more second-rate Christianity!* That was it! During the next two hours, I cried that sentence, I shouted it, I sang it; it seethed through my teeth, it leapt off my heart.

Over the next two weeks, five major families left our church. Like most congregations with a weekly attendance of around one hundred, we simply could not afford that loss. Yet they left. I was confused, for I had changed nothing. Yet they sensed a change anyway and decided they did not like it. On the third Sunday after my labor on the mountain, all heaven broke loose during the worship service. People began crying spontaneously. Others were healed. All were obviously in love with God. God was there and everybody knew it. The whole atmosphere was charged with His presence and power. And, with periodic fluctuations in intensity, it has been that way ever since.

I will never go back to second-rate Christianity, but precious few congregations really want first-rate Christianity. First-rate religion requires vulnerability to God. I am perfectly content to remain at St. Jude's for the rest of my days, for God told me clearly that I was to spend myself within the Episcopal Church. God has taken away my fear of being vulnerable and replaced it with a determination to benefit His Kingdom, come what may.

There is joy in no longer running one's life and, therefore, being truly responsible. The most responsible act is to let the Responsible One run things. The joy comes from knowing that you are in collaboration with Someone really huge, really effective, really competent, really free. There is a rightness about being vulnerable to God that satisfies deeply. Something within us rises up and shouts, "Yes!" because we know that we are finally on the right track.

Part of that joy comes of trusting God with things that really count. We have been created to flourish in an attitude of trust. Trust releases a satisfaction that is deeper than mere comfort. It is as though each of us possesses at the bottom of our souls an artesian well waiting to be tapped. Active trust allows God to fill us up from the depths of our beings with the living waters promised by our Savior.

Another benefit of vulnerability to God is that it provides experiential proof of God's love, guidance, provision and Lordship. God does not *have* love; He *is* love. Being vulnerable to Him is being vulnerable to love, and the nice thing about love is that it ceaselessly seeks the benefit of the beloved.

The Old Testament names for God disclose this dynamic. *Jehovah*, you recall, is a name that revolves around itself: *I am what I am what I am*, etc. In other words: *I am* reality itself. Then, seven times, *Jehovah* is hyphenated with other words.[1] *Jehovah-ra'ah* means "*I am* your shepherd. Do you need shepherding? Then you need Me," God says. *Jehovah-tsidkenu:* "*I am* your righteousness. Do you need righteousness? Then you need Me." *Jehovah-jireh:* "*I am* your supply. Do you need something? Then you need Me." There is even good grammatical evidence that *Jesus* is the Greek form of a shortened

---

[1] I am indebted to Roy and Revel Hession for these passages, first encountered in their book *We Would See Jesus.*

Jehovah-jireh, Genesis 22:14. *I am* your provider.
Jehovah-nissi, Exodus 17:15. *I am* your banner.
Jehovah-shalom, Judges 6:24. *I am* your peace.
Jehovah-ra'ah, Psalm 23:1. *I am* your shepherd.
Jehovah-rapha, Exodus 15:26. *I am* your healer.
Jehovah-tsidkenu, Jeremiah 23:6. *I am* your righteousness.
Jehovah-shammah, Ezekiel 48:35. *I am* the one who is present.

Hebrew word meaning "*I am* your salvation." "Do you need saving? Then you need Me."

It is as though the Lord gives these names to us as a means of prompting us to realize that His name is *I Am* _____ (you fill in the blank). Vulnerability to *I Am* _____ exposes us to the divine need-filler. That means we are also exposed to His will, His timing and His conditions. And that, of course, is where our woundability comes in. But my testimony, and that of thousands through the ages, is that God wounds us for our own benefit and in ways that we *agree* were for our benefit, once we reflect on them.

Notice that agreement comes *after the fact.* At the moment, it is rare for us to see clearly enough to agree that a challenge is for our benefit. It is only when we have obeyed, seen the outcome and reflected on the whole experience that we can agree that the event was for our benefit from the start.

What gets wounded in an encounter with vulnerability? *Ego* is first on the list: God sees pride as such a nuisance. But "wounded" is not the same as "destroyed." I have never had my pride fatally injured, nor has God seen fit to humiliate me publicly. That is an interesting point: Often the wounding of my ego comes in public settings, but the public almost never notices the wounding; it seems noticeable only to God and myself.

Self-confidence is another factor that gets wounded. Death to self-confidence rebirths me into God-confidence.

Self-effort is another woundable. Its wounding is the first step in the reduction of fatigue. If I cannot do anything anyway, then I don't waste energy trying. For a long time I had to confess self-effort each night before I dropped out of fatigue and into sleep. What I was doing was *adding* my own agenda to the Lord's. If I had done just what He directed, I wouldn't have been fatigued at night, but I didn't trust Him

to cover all the bases. The wounding of self-effort was a
lengthy process, which I hope has been largely concluded.

Fleshly competence is another woundable. This differs from
self-effort in that it is a reliance upon the flesh to accomplish
what has been heard in the Spirit. One can hear from God
what he is to do, but fall back on human ability and resource
to accomplish the task. This can be frustrating, because nothing turns out right. The wounding of fleshly competence is
painful largely because we don't understand what is going on.
The confusion hurts. "Here You tell me what to do, God, and
I do it and the thing turns out horribly." But when the wounding gets to a certain point, we realize suddenly that we need
God's power and resources in order to accomplish God's directives. Then things get better.

Tradition is an eminent woundable. Jesus had not-good
things to say about the "traditions of men." "Well, *our* traditions aren't of men but of God," we may reply. Look out! It
takes only three short generations for something of God to
become His enemy in the hands of men. Tradition is probably
the greatest hurdle for God to deal with in the contemporary
Church. Traditions compete with God because they supplant
Him; we depend on them. If He cannot get us to abandon
them, He must be sorely provoked to "wipe the dust of them"
off His feet before finding someone who is not bound and can
respond to Him.

Am I saying that traditions are bad? That depends entirely
on the manner of those practicing them. First-generation re-
sponsiveness rapidly gives way to third-generation medioc-
rity. That is a proven sociological reality and the primary
reason for the constant need for renewal. It has become a
truism, in fact, to say that the renewal is in need of renewal.

Vulnerability to God is the major dynamic that counteracts
the tendency to make traditions and become bound to them.

It is impossible not to make traditions. Their roles are generally positive, but tradition does insinuate itself into the role of God, and we sin when we collaborate with it.

Trusting a tradition is much simpler and more comfortable than trusting God. We have even found ourselves institutionalizing our conferences on how to respond to the Spirit. The only thing that saves us is when we say, "Come, Holy Spirit," because you never know what He is going to do. It would not surprise me if He told us to stop saying, "Come, Holy Spirit," for we have the ability to institutionalize even that.

Vulnerability is a lifestyle. It is not a phase. It is not a stage. It is not a temporary time of testing. It is not what you do for a while until you have graduated. It is what's before us for the duration.

A final woundable is *life*. We all know many stories of martyrdom from past centuries, and we assume those days are over. But researchers estimate that there are a hundred thousand new martyrs every year worldwide. Stories coming out of East Africa and China over the past decade are full of the vulnerability and glory of martyrdom.

It might seem strange to write of martyrdom in a nice, unthreatening little book like this. But I believe that I have a prediction for the Church in America today: If we experiment seriously with vulnerability to God, we will find the rate of martyrdom accelerating rapidly in our country. Somewhere in my spirit I feel that soon there will be deaths among protesters of the practice of abortion. They will be but the firstfruits of a spilling of blood that will be the seed of the replanting of the Gospel in this land.

Martyrdom is a spiritual gift. That is, there comes a grace to those selected for it that is magnificent. They manifest wonderful, victorious peace; they show Jesus' own forgiveness toward their persecutors; they comfort those who come to comfort them. But it is not so magnificent as to lead us to suppose that martyrdom is abnormal. It is not all that unusual. We just have not been vital enough recently in this country to call it forth from the enemy.

In the meantime, we can practice with laying down another kind of life. "Greater love," Jesus said, "has no one than this, that one lay down his life for his friends" (John 15:13). The word for *life* here is not *zoe*, physical life, but *psyche*, soul-life. Remember that the soul is made up of mind and emotions. To lay down one's life for one's friends is to give up what we think and how we feel, for their sake. Now how is that for a challenge? To forgo opinions and to quiet emotions in order to love our friends—that is excellent preparation for laying down our physical lives, should the opportunity ever come.

So many "recent studies" would argue against surrendering our opinions and "stuffing" our emotions that there must be some other reasonable interpretation of Jesus' words. Perhaps. But you will never know if He really meant what He said if you don't give it a shot. You don't have to do it for the whole world, just your friends. How about it? If this book has said anything of interest to you, maybe you would be willing to put it to action at this point. How about a six-month experiment in which you withhold your negative opinions of your friends and refuse to express your negative emotions as a means by which to greatly love them?

In the next and final chapter, we will review briefly what has been said about vulnerability. Then we will think about an agenda God may have for extending vulnerability into our individual and corporate lives in order to accomplish something significant for the Church and nation today. We will conclude with a comment about vulnerability we may not have yet anticipated.

13
Vulnerability to Mystery

As I listened to her catalog the ills in her life, my heart sank. *My God!* I thought. *Any* one *of these will take monumental amounts of work to fix. How will we ever deal with all of them?*

Then I heard clearly the instructions, *Go over and sit beside her and pray out loud in tongues.* So I did. At first, I was kind of bored because, as Paul notes, when you pray in the Spirit your mind is "unfruitful" (1 Corinthians 14:14). But after a couple minutes, I saw in my mind's eye a dense fog, which obstructed my view of anything else. After a time, the fog thinned enough for me to see Jesus with His back to me, perhaps ten feet away. In front of Him was a dentist's chair with someone reclining in it. I gathered that it was this woman. Jesus was making motions as though He were operating on her midsection. Then the fog swirled to close the scene. A few minutes later, the fog cleared to reveal Jesus still at work, then closed once again.

I happened to look at my watch. I had been praying for seven minutes. As I began to try to determine which of the woman's many problems we should start on, I noticed that she was getting ready to leave.

"What are you doing?" I asked.

"I'm going home," was her reply, apparently surprised that I should ask.

"Why?" I said. It made no sense that, after detailing the horrendous list of things that were wrong, she would suddenly make ready to leave.

"Well, I'm O.K. now."

"What do you mean?" I said, astonished. "What happened?"

She pursed her face, paused for a very long time and then said, "I can't tell you." She tucked her purse under her arm, said goodbye and left.

After that, whenever I asked her what had happened that day, she would purse her face, struggle to find some way to articulate, give it up as a lost cause and say, "I can't tell you." Not all of her problems were over, but something quite extraordinary had occurred that day. When I finally got around to asking the Lord—getting no satisfaction from her—He said, *None of your business.* Case closed!

Well, the case may have been closed for *Him,* but it wasn't yet closed for me until I changed my attitude about mystery.

There is a drive in our society to unravel the unknown. It comes of our Western worldview. Also, much in Scripture commends this drive to understand. Some years ago, if my memory serves me accurately, I counted fourteen times in Paul's letters where this phrase occurred, *That you may understand.*

But *understand* does not always mean in Scripture what we think it should mean in Western thought. Let's look at some passages on mystery.

> To them God has chosen to make known among the Gentiles the glorious riches of this *mystery,* which is Christ in you, the hope of glory.
>
> Colossians 1:27

This is a profound *mystery*—but I am talking about Christ and the church.

Ephesians 5:32

Listen, I tell you a *mystery:* We will not all sleep, but we will all be changed.

1 Corinthians 15:51

. . . According to the revelation of the *mystery* hidden for long ages past, but now revealed and made known through the prophetic writings by the command of the eternal God, so that all nations might believe and obey him.

Romans 16:25–26

Beyond all question, the *mystery* of godliness is great: He appeared in a body, was vindicated by the Spirit.

1 Timothy 3:16

All of these passages were written by the same fellow who hoped "that you may understand." But notice something about the use of "mystery" in these texts:

- Mystery can be made known
- Mystery can be talked about
- Mysteries can be told

But mysteries remain mysterious. To tell a mystery does not suddenly change its nature so that it is no longer mysterious. To reveal a mystery does not strip it of its mysteriousness. We have read so many whodunits that we expect real mysteries to comply obediently with our need to know and come out of hiding. If they don't, we are tempted to label them nonsense, unreality, fiction—none of which we take seriously.

Does saying that mysteries remain mysterious exempt us from examining them, meditating on them, probing them and seeking to understand them with all our human and divine resources? Of course not. Probing the mysterious is a central quest.

What I am getting at is the *attitude* with which we consider mystery. If we are hostile toward mystery, it has an uncanny way of receding. This is what happened to me in the episode with John 3 in which I was going to crack open the truth of that passage. My intent had been to strip it of its wonder, digest its features and notch the handle of my mental gun in the satisfaction that another truth had bowed to my prowess.

But if we come to mystery—to God and the things of God—with an attitude of humility, then mysteries tend to open to us.

I have tried in the previous chapters of this book to share some of the things that God places between us and Him. The manner in which we deal with these things determines the quality of our relationship with Him. Reviewing these things for a moment may prepare us for the concluding comments.

Interacting with God

Biblical anthropology is one of the factors to which we are invited to be vulnerable. God's Word is saying, *"This* is how you are put together, *this* is how you have been designed to function." We can benefit from secular theories about humankind, but they must augment the scriptural view or be set aside. A few years ago a young man came to me because he was about to lose his job in a Christian organization. He lost his temper consistently. After interviewing him I concluded that he was suffering from a spirit of anger. After explaining to him what this meant, I asked for his permission to address that spirit to tell it to leave.

Some spirits put up a real fight, but this one was so mild I wasn't sure it had left. A Christian psychologist called me several weeks later, telling me that he had been treating the young man for about six months and had noticed a radical change since his meeting with me. He wanted to know what I had done and how I had done it so quickly, so we set up a lunch meeting. I explained what I had done, and we dialogued about the issue for a while. Then I looked over his head at Jesus, a practice I described in chapter 11. I was led to challenge him: Was he first a psychologist who was also a Christian or first a Christian who was also a psychologist?

He left unable to answer the question. After all, he had spent years of intense study obtaining his Ph.D., which had invested him heavily in a psychological worldview. But I kept track of him through some mutual acquaintances. About two years after our lunch, I learned that he had become a Christian who was also a psychologist and was in demand as an especially effective counselor. He is now teaching psychology very effectively in a university, having proven to himself that the Bible's anthropology takes precedence over any other.

Vulnerability to Scripture

This takes us to the chapter on Scripture. Being vulnerable to Scripture does not mean literalism or liberalism, neither of which requires much mental or spiritual vulnerability. It means discovering and then adopting Jesus' attitude toward and utilization of Scripture. The God of the Word is so lively that His Word is also lively. As we submit ourselves to the

Word's vitality, we come into the presence of the One who is vitality itself.

Vulnerability to Discomfort

To do this with consistency and integrity involves us in a reconciliation with discomfort. If we do not achieve that reconciliation, we will compromise the integrity with which we approach the Lord and His Word. To be idolatrous toward comfort is to be hostile to the ways of God. We are always a bit off-balance if we are dealing effectively with the living God. So be it.

Vulnerability to Jesus' Worldview

Coming to a willful adoption of Jesus' worldview is a vulnerability we will endure all our lives, for His riches are "unsearchable" (Ephesians 3:8). If your intellectual pride demands that you know everything, you will be tempted to replace Jesus' viewpoint with your own. This affects your love for Him and your understanding of His love for you. But submitting to His way of seeing things frees you "to know this love that surpasses knowledge—that you may be filled to the measure of all the fullness of God" (Ephesians 3:19).

Vulnerability to the Headship of Jesus

Opening ourselves to the headship of Jesus means taking seriously Jesus' relationship with the Father as the model for our relationship with Him. How can we ever begin to live up to such a high standard? By operating in the same Spirit as Jesus under the same obedience for the same ends. "To obey is better than sacrifice" (1 Samuel 15:22, Proverbs 21:3) because you can sacrifice without vulnerability to God, but you cannot obey without it.

Vulnerability to Self

Vulnerability to self takes seriously the creative and incarnational and redemptive genius of God. He has created me thus. He reveals Himself in me just as I am now. Thus I must embrace myself in Him or slander Him.

Vulnerability to Spiritual Warfare

Vulnerability to spiritual warfare is accepting the primary dynamic affecting our planet. You may need to say, "Well, Lord, I would rather be a spiritual pacifist, but You allow no such role. So I agree that I am a soldier rather than a spectator. I suit up in Your equipment and go forth to Your frays. Teach me how to fight. Extend Your Kingdom through me."

Vulnerability to Guidance

Getting accurate guidance is a matter of great importance, so long as we don't allow it to interfere with the requirement to have faith. Guidance needs to be confirmed, but that doesn't mean that mistakes are eliminated. Learning the manner in which God speaks and risking action based on that word—ah, that is vulnerability to the nines.

Vulnerability to God's "Collective" View of His People

Letting God see us in the corporate; having the ability to influence each other for good and for ill; accepting the oneness of humankind—these require a special vulnerability. To have such influence on others! To be so influenced by them! Communality requires trust in the ability of our God to administrate "plans to prosper you and not to harm you, plans to give you hope and a future" (Jeremiah 29:11). God can make His collective view of people work for us.

Vulnerability to Authority

Having and being under authority can wound us. Vulnerability to authority means trusting God to help us both use and submit to the authority He has brought into our lives. What's more, it means trusting Him to handle the mishandling of authority and bring the whole thing right. Authority is a necessary ingredient of communality, so we'd better learn how to use it effectively.

Vulnerability to the Presence of Jesus

Being vulnerable to the presence of Jesus can be an upper and a downer. Look at Peter's experience in Caesarea Philippi. Jesus said, "Who do you say I am?" Peter had the grace to check in with the Father, who inspired him to reply, "You are the Christ, the Son of the living God." And that is exactly what Jesus commended him for: "Blessed are you, Simon son of Jonah, for this was not revealed to you by man, but by my Father in heaven" (Matthew 16:15–17). A real upper.

Now that they know who He is, Jesus begins telling them what He has to do: "From that time on Jesus began to explain to his disciples that he must go to Jerusalem and suffer many things" (verse 21). But Peter stopped checking in with the Father and answered out of the flesh, "Never, Lord! . . . This shall never happen to you!" (verse 22).

Jesus' rebuke came swiftly: "Out of my sight, Satan! You

are a stumbling block to me; you do not have in mind the things of God, but the things of men" (verse 23). A real downer.

Vulnerability to the presence of Jesus is a wonderful blessing when you are walking in dependence on the Spirit, and it can be a real trial when you are depending on yourself, which we all do from time to time. Jesus' presence involves openness to the power of the Spirit, to love, to seeing, to contemporaneity, to prayer and to His enthronement in all situations.

Meeting Our Needs through Vulnerability

The healing of vulnerability comes out of a mental shift by which we begin to see weakness as strength when our weakness is the platform on which the living God operates through us. Vulnerability is not to be endured but embraced. Vulnerability says to God, "I'm putting You first," to which God can reply, "Ah, you have freed Me to bless you."

God uses these dynamics to bring us to Himself. God lurks close behind the things of God.

Peter said something extraordinary in his second letter:

> His divine power has given us everything we need for life and godliness through our knowledge of him who called us by his own glory and goodness. Through these he has given us his very great and precious promises, so that through them you may *participate in the divine nature* and escape the corruption in the world caused by evil desires.
>
> 2 Peter 1:3–4

To "participate in the divine nature" does not mean that we become transformed into deity, but that we have fellowship with Him. The italicized phrase is in Greek *Theias* (divine) *koinoonoi* (sharers) *physeoos* (nature); most readers will recognize the word for fellowship, *koinonia*, in the word translated as "participate." The word meaning "nature," *physis*, has reference to God's character, rather than His essence. The Godhead is a community of Persons in flawless relationship with one another.

Thus to participate in the divine nature is to come into the fullness of the Trinity. "Come on in!" is what God says about the community of His three-part Personhood. Peter tells us how to come in:

> For this very reason, make every effort to add to your faith goodness; and to goodness, knowledge; and to knowledge, self-control; and to self-control, perseverance; and to perseverance, godliness; and to godliness, brotherly kindness; and to brotherly kindness, love.
>
> 2 Peter 1:5–7

These qualities bear a strong resemblance to what Paul calls "the fruit of the Spirit."[1] What are the fruit of the Spirit? They are Jesus' character made available to believers through the operation of the Holy Spirit. What do the fruit do? They counteract the tendencies of the flesh on a moment-by-moment basis.

Remember in chapter 1 what happened when I asked God to kill my pride? He said, No way, that to do so would reduce my need for Him. If God killed my pride, I would be able to go off and be humble on my own, without reference to Him. Since He created me for relationship with Him, He was not

---

[1] "But the fruit of the Spirit is love, joy, peace, patience, kindness, goodness, faithfulness, gentleness and self-control" (Galatians 5:22–23).

about to do something that would diminish our relationship. Does He want me to be humble? Absolutely. But He has His own method of achieving that humility, namely, unbroken fellowship with Him through His Spirit.

If I put you into a room that had no windows and closed the door, it would be dark in that room, whether it was day or night. If you turned on the light, the light would counteract the darkness on a second-by-second basis. As soon as you switched *off* the light, the darkness would reassert itself instantly. The flesh is our tendency toward darkness, and the Holy Spirit is the light.

If you depend on the Holy Spirit to counteract your tendencies toward darkness by giving you the character of Jesus on a continuous basis, you have nothing to fear from the flesh. But if you presume to be able to defeat the darkness on your own—outside of the divine community—it is going to defeat you again and again.

God's appointed means by which we can have direct relationship with Him is His own Spirit. It could not be otherwise. This is why such incredible things happen when we say, "Come, Holy Spirit"—because we are asking for the unmediated presence of God Himself, and He Himself shows up. The Spirit is neither so transcendent that He would not visit you nor so immanent that He neglects galaxies. This is why it is so thrilling: The God who moves in the outermost void is the same God who visits you at your invitation. How astoundingly humble of Him! "What is man, that You are mindful of him?" is the way the psalmist exclaimed it.

Does *all* of God show up when we say, "Come, Holy Spirit"? Yes and no. The "yes" is that the fullness of God visits us, not the extent of God. You get all of God; anyone else anywhere at the same time can get all of Him, too.

The "no" is that He is limited by our ability to receive

Him. A couple of months ago a young pastor came to ask if I would pray for him. As I checked with the Lord, I offered to pray for several things, including the infilling of the Holy Spirit, none of which he wanted. I was on the verge of saying, "Look, young man, why don't you go home and ask God what He wants to give you, and then come back," but suddenly he blurted out, "I want to heal the sick." As I checked with the Lord, He released me to pray, giving the young man an anointing for healing. There was so much more that he could have received, I thought, as he left the office.

Later he came back. God had started healing people he prayed for, and he was ashamed. Of what? His past sins. So he made a life confession of sin, beseeching Jesus to cleanse him so that God's power could go through him unstained. Then he felt ready to receive more of what God had for him. In his case, he could not ask for much at first. Others can ask for much but not receive it because they are not ready yet.

On an individual and communal level, God is unable to give all His blessings because we are not prepared. James said that a double-minded man can't receive *anything* from God (1:6–8). Why? Because whatever God gave him would capsize him until he brought himself to singlemindedness.

Many in the Church today are praying for revival. Praise God! It is the great need of the Church and the land today. But in order to answer, God is going to have to send—and we are going to have to receive—a series of gifts:

Cleansing. When God withholds His grace because we are dirty, it isn't punishment—He already punished His Son in our places. It is to relieve us of the enemy's counterattack that we would be unable to sustain; it is to save us from capsizing under the weight of blessing (blessing *does* weigh). So cleansing is necessary in order for many prayers to be answered.

Repentance is both a process and an event. It is a *process* in that we are unable to deal with more than one behavior at a time. Conviction, confession and amendment generally focus on one behavior at a time. We may be sorry for all kinds of acts, but they generally get cured one at a time. Repentance is an *event* in that you don't have to keep on confessing the same sin. You get convicted of it, you become sorry for it, you ask God to forgive you for it, you appropriate His forgiveness and it's over.

Because you can deal with only one behavior at a time, cleansing is a process that may take months to accomplish. I have known whole congregations that were in repentance for a year at a time.

Faith. When the people asked Jesus in John 6 what they should work for, He replied that their job was to believe in the one the Father had sent (verse 29). Without seeing the outcome in advance, we are going to have to believe in the Son and the validity of the things He is telling us to do. We are going to have to take seriously the current words, following them as best we can and leaving the results up to the Lord.

Commitment. Commitment is always a choice between the things of God and the things of the world. Our present affection for material goods may be the do-or-die for most Christians in our nation today. If God starts challenging us to separate ourselves from the world, we may find out exactly how much we honor His commands. If He requires separation, we shouldn't be too surprised, for the word *holy* means separated.

Power. It is time we stopped playing charismatic games. Charismatic games are centered on discussions of whether certain experiences are for today or not. The young pastor mentioned earlier in this chapter did not want to be filled with the Holy Spirit. If I had insisted that he be filled before he was anointed for healing, which I nearly did, he would not be healing the sick today. If the Holy Spirit was kind enough to anoint the household of Cornelius with tongues and prophecy before they had even been saved, why can't we let Him do the same today?

Wherever people can allow themselves to collaborate with God's power, let's let them. Once people begin working with the Holy Spirit, they are soon open to more. Almost everyone I have seen go into the healing ministry is soon filled with the Spirit. Why? Because when you are face to face with someone whose illness is beyond your ability to help, your compassion quickly turns you to whatever power might be available.

Humility. There is much being spoken on the front lines of the Church today about humility. The reason is that many church leaders have supplanted God as the proper recipient of glory and esteem. Something in us, I think, winces when a ministry is called by the name of the minister. If the minister has the humility not to have his head turned by a ministry named for him, those following him may not.

One prophetic vision spoken today foretells coliseums filled with people being healed and converted by leaders who are so humble that the press can't find them to talk to or even discover what their names are.

What is God saying about glory? Two things, I think. First, "I am the Lord; that is my name! I will not give my glory to another or my praise to idols" (Isaiah 42:8). Mere men have taken to themselves commendations meant for God. God doesn't give His glory to others because they don't have the humility to sustain it.

Second, "And we, who with unveiled faces all reflect the Lord's glory, are being transformed into his likeness with ever-increasing glory, which comes from the Lord, who is the Spirit" (2 Corinthians 3:18). *Intercepted glory capsizes us, but reflected glory transforms us.* God alone is responsible for all that is good—even Jesus said, "Why do you call Me good?"—and that frees us to be changed into His likeness.

Procedure. David Ravenhill, in a recent conference on holiness, noted that King David, with all good intentions, displeased God when he brought the Ark into Jerusalem because he had not inquired of the Lord for the proper procedure.[2] God has a way for each of His things to be done, and we must let Him require them of us. Is He God or is He not?

The foregoing list daunts me. I have not "arrived" in any of these areas. At the same time, I know that God is calling, beckoning to His people to shrug off less than life and go on to real life, which is God Himself. In order to encourage you to hope in His ability to bring you further into His glory, I want to tell you a story on myself.

As I indicated earlier, I have a problem keeping covenant with my eyes. It is a common problem among men, who are more visually oriented. Being married is a great help to men with this problem, but it is not a cure, for other needs than marriage are the root of the illness. Once Sue and our boys had gone to another city to visit friends. I was rattling around in the house one evening with a vague unrest gnawing at me, for I was fighting a picture that had been in my mind for a couple of weeks. It was the cover of a magazine. I had seen it in a nearby store and had let my eyes dwell on it long enough to imprint in on my memory.

I decided suddenly to go and buy that magazine. Now

---

[2] David failed to inquire of God. He built a cart to transport the Ark, forgetting or failing to allow God to remind him that the Ark had to be carried on men's shoulders. God's very presence requires a higher standard of response from us than the things of God, which can be transported on carts. See 1 Chronicles 13 and 15.

normally when I have decided to sin, God is the last person I want to talk with. I have a knack for putting on blinders, bending my head and dashing straight for the sin. I know I will talk with Him later, when the guilt sets in, but at the moment I am given to sin.

This time, however, I decided to talk to Him. I didn't have much time to talk, for the store was just two blocks away. But as I walked toward it, I said, "I'm sorry, Lord, but I'm going to buy that magazine. I have let the enemy set a hook in me with that magazine cover and he's yanking on it and I have been caught. If You can block me, go ahead. But You are going to have to do it, because I have caved in to the temptation."

As I walked into the store, I made a beeline for the magazine rack. I was just about to reach up and take the magazine when I heard my name called.

I cursed inwardly, turning to see who had hailed me. It was a young man who had been coming to our church for several months. Then he came out of the checkout line to chat. And for several moments he chatted amiably about several things, while I inwardly chafed, hoping he would leave so I could buy the magazine.

Then he grew serious and pulled me off to the side so as to ensure confidentiality and said, "I've got something bothering me and I wonder if you'd help me with it. [Pause. Deep breath.] How do you handle temptation?"

I would like to say that I dropped to my knees crying out to God for mercy, but I didn't. Instead, I began giving him my standard spiel on how to handle temptation.[3] The difference was that I gave it as fast as I possibly could. He seemed genuinely encouraged by what I said. Finally he looked at his watch, got back into the checkout line and left.

[3] See chapter 7.

For a moment I just stood there. "You rat," I said to the Lord, with resignation and a hint of amusement. For it was dawning on me that the things I had told the young man were true, were real and were effective. Having told him, I had told myself as well. So I turned my head toward the door and walked out. Before I got back home, I was in glory. What an incredible God! What an incredible God whose arm is never short and who is never through with us! What incredible largeness of Spirit, to hang in with me when I was bent on disobeying Him, to befriend me when I was acting exactly like a sworn enemy!

Keep on talking to Me, son, He said. *If you keep talking, you maintain a connection I can work with. Never stop talking to Me.* One reason I can be vulnerable to Him is that He is vulnerable to me. All through this book I have been talking about *our* vulnerability to *Him*. But behind all that has been *His* vulnerability to *us*.

The Vulnerability of God

How is God vulnerable to us? I think the first way is that He promises never to leave or abandon us. If anyone has a *right* to leave us, it is God. But He promises not to exercise that option, even though it must cost Him a lot. He states, for example, that He knows everything that we do, think or say. That requires close proximity to us. He who is purity itself refuses to leave us though we do things that are impure. He refuses to leave, to look the other way, to close His eyes or even to wish He were somewhere else. In other words, His commitment to stay with us involves Him in vulnerability to our impurity.

Second, He promises to hear our prayers. There are conditions necessary for the *answering* of our prayers, but, apparently, not on hearing them. Though we may feel that our prayers are not penetrating the ceiling, He promises to hear us every time. You don't have to go to Him in order to be heard, for He is always within earshot of you. So He is vulnerable to our presence.

And how about the vulnerability of Jesus, "who ever lives to make intercession for us" (Hebrews 7:25)? If anyone has deserved a break from ministering to man, it is Jesus. But He chooses to keep on ministering to us by interceding for us continually. He doesn't take breaks, vacations or naps. He is constantly doing the hard work of interceding for our needs, opportunities, dangers and eternal destinies. So He is vulnerable to our needs.

Forgiveness places God at great vulnerability. He has paid the dearest price imaginable in order to satisfy the demands of justice—*someone* had to pay for what we have done—while freeing Him to fulfill His yearning for mercy upon us. When we confess, He truly and completely forgives. When we go out and sin again, He has bound Himself to forgive again. And again. He has pledged that He will forgive. Every time. Think how that places Him at vulnerability to us. He never protects Himself from the possibility of our hurting Him again. So He is vulnerable to our sins.

Think of divine love. He makes Himself vulnerable to us by placing the responsibility for our acceptability on Himself, rather than on us. God doesn't love you because you deserve it; He loves you because He is a lover. If you could deserve His love, it would cease being a gift and would become payment. But God Himself insists that His love is a gift; therefore, He places the basis for our acceptability on Himself, not on us. He pledges to love us whether or not we ever deserve His love. So He is vulnerable to the possibility of unrequited love.

As someone once said, "In the final analysis there are only two kinds of people: those who say to God, 'Thy will be done,' and those to whom God says, 'Thy will be done.' " So He is vulnerable to our free will by which we accept or reject His plan. He will take us to heaven or allow us to take ourselves to hell. Think of the eternal agony He will suffer, pining for those who have rejected His offer.

Finally, our vulnerability involves us in sin, partial conformity to His will, confusion, disobedience, resourceless idealism, sheer self-centeredness and countless mistakes. Yet God still hangs in with us, still hears us, still loves us, still makes plans for us, still cherishes and accepts and forgives and restarts us. So He is vulnerable to our vulnerability.

You see, He believes in His love for us. He believes that if He keeps on loving us, we will get the message. And then we will change. Not in order to win something. That has already been given. But in thanksgiving for what we have already received.

He who is continually losing His life for us believes that He will get it back. He gets it back when we are vulnerable to Him. And we get it back yet again, as a reward for following Him.

The key is this: *Whom would you rather receive from—yourself or God?* If you are holding onto your life, you are receiving from yourself. But if you are losing your life, you are receiving from God—who can give to you much better than you can. Gain through loss; strength through weakness; receptivity through giving; answers through faith; healing through vulnerability. It is the dynamic of life.

When a wound comes into an oyster—a speck of sand or a breach—all the resources of repair are rushed to it.[4] Had there

4 *Streams in the Desert* by Mrs. Charles E. Cowman.

been no wound, those resources would never have been discovered. After a long process, the result is a beautiful pearl. ("When he found one of great value, he went away and sold everything he had and bought it" Matthew 13:46.) The deep, rich, luminous beauty of the pearl would never have been seen had there been no wound. No wound, no pearl. Each of the twelve gates into the heavenly Jerusalem is a single pearl.[5] No wound, no entrance into heaven.

Jesus Christ suffered agonizing wounds. His cure is the entrance into the place of healing for us, "by whose stripes you have been healed." He promises His cure to all who follow. Vulnerability to God is His doorway.

[5] Revelation 21:21.